The EARLY Intervention Kit™

Nancy B. Swigert

Skill: Language
Ages: Birth–3 years

LinguiSystems, Inc.
3100 4th Avenue
East Moline, IL 61244

800-776-4332

FAX: 800-577-4555
E-mail: service@linguisystems.com
Web: linguisystems.com

Copyright © 2004 LinguiSystems, Inc.

All of our products are copyrighted to protect the fine work of our authors. You may only copy the client materials as needed for your own use with clients. Any other reproduction or distribution of the pages in this book is prohibited, including copying the entire book to use as another primary source or "master" copy.

Printed in the U.S.A.
ISBN 10: 0-7606-0596-3
ISBN 13: 978-0-7606-0596-7

About the Author

Nancy B. Swigert, M.A., CCC-SLP, received her master's degree from the University of Tennessee, Knoxville. She is the president of Swigert & Associates, Inc., a private practice that has been providing services in the Lexington, Kentucky area for over 25 years. The practice provides early intervention services in child care and home settings and through their contractual arrangement with Central Baptist Hospital. In addition to administering the private practice, Nancy spends much of her time providing patient care. She provides services to young children and adults with feeding and swallowing disorders and to medically fragile infants and toddlers with communication delays and disorders.

Nancy also lectures across the country on topics, that include adult and pediatric dysphagia, reading disorders, dysarthria, developmental apraxia, and evidence-based practice. This is her fifth publication with LinguiSystems. Her other books are *The Source for Dysphagia*, *The Source for Pediatric Dysphagia*, *The Source for Dysarthria*, and *The Source for Reading Fluency*.

Nancy served as president of the American Speech-Language-Hearing Association in 1998 and continues to be very involved with ASHA, currently serving as chair of the Health Care Economics Committee and on the Steering Committee for Special Interest Division 13: Swallowing and Swallowing Disorders. She is currently President of the American Speech-Language-Hearing Foundation.

Edited by Lauri Whiskeyman
Cover design by Mike Paustian and Lisa Parker
Page layout by Denise L. Kelly
Sign language alphabet, numbers, and some vocabulary pictures illustrated by Margaret Warner.
The rest of the sign language vocabulary pictures are reprinted with permission from
A Basic Course in Manual Communication, Communicative Skills Program, Terrence J. O'Rourke, Director
The National Association of the Deaf © 1973.

The blissymbol on page 128 was reprinted with permission. Blissymbol used herein derived from the symbols described in the work *Semantography*, original copyright © C. K. Bliss 1949. In September, 1982, C. K. Bliss granted an exclusive, non-cancellable, and perpetual worldwide license to the Blissymbolics Communication International for the application of Blissymbols for use by handicapped persons and persons having communication, language, and learning difficulties.

Acknowledgments

This book would not have been possible without the combined efforts of all of the speech-language pathologists in my practice who provide early intervention services. Special thanks to the following who authored chapters and/or sections in this kit:

Jennifer Perry Blevins, M.S., CCC-SLP—Chapter 11: Augmentative and Alternative Communication and the parent handouts in the *Activities Book*

Sarah Shoemaker Shields, M.S., CCC-SLP—Chapter 4: Medical Disorders and Syndromes Associated with Children Birth to Three

Verity Mathews, M.S., CCC-SLP—Activities for expressive language in the *Activities Book*

And to the following for contributing significantly by writing many of the activities in the *Activities Book*:

Julie Bourne, M.A., CCC-SLP
Kim Gray Helmuth, M.S., CCC-SLP
Ashley Kemp Orr, M.S., CCC-SLP

Michelle Lankster, M.S., CCC-SLP
Sarah Richardson Crain, M.A., CCC-SLP
Lissa Wellman Stephens, M.A., CCC-SLP

Two other employees of my practice also made significant contributions:

Geri Cobb, Executive Assistant, provided invaluable direction in the organization and structure of this kit.

Melinda Spurlock compiled and typed many of the activities and found and cross-checked all of our references.

(top row - left to right) Kim Gray Helmuth, Michelle Lankster, Nancy Swigert, Sarah Richardson Crain
(middle row - left to right) Julie Bourne, Lissa Wellman Stephens, Ashley Kemp Orr
(front row - left to right) Sarah Shoemaker Shields, Verity Mathews, Jennifer Perry Blevins

Table of Contents

Introduction 9

Chapter 1: The Evolution of Early Intervention 11
Traditional Curriculum Models 11
Naturalistic Model 12

Chapter 2: Unique Features of Service Delivery 14
Service Delivery Model 14
Child Characteristics and Needs 20
Treatment Planning 23
Appendix 2A: *Hawaii Preparing for Integrated Preschool* (PIP) Assessment 25

Chapter 3: Evidence Base for Early Intervention 29
Effectiveness of Early Intervention 29
Effectiveness of Types of Intervention 30
Examples of Research with Specific Populations 32

Chapter 4: Medical Disorders and Syndromes Associated with Children Birth to Three .. 36
Chromosomal/Genetic Disorders 36
Neurological Disorders 39
Congenital Malformations 40
Atypical Development 41
Environmental Disorders and Other Medical Factors 42
Sensory Disorders 44
Infectious Diseases 45
Appendix 4A: Resources 46

Chapter 5: Tools and Methods for Assessment 47
What Is Assessment? 47
Principles of Assessment 48
Home-based vs. Center-based Assessments 50
Models of Assessment 51
Areas to Assess 51
Types of Tests 56
Adjusting for Prematurity 58
Hearing Acuity 58
Reassessing/Measuring Progress 58
Appendix 5A: Examples of Tests for Birth-to-Three Population 61
Appendix 5B: Symbolic Play Scale Checklist 65

Chapter 6: Treatment Methods, Techniques, and Materials 66
Activity-based Instruction 66
A Partnership Model: Following the Child's Lead 67
Effective Consequences 69
Remediation, Redefinition, and Re-education 71
Treatment Materials 72
Appendix 6A: Suggested Toys, Materials, and Books for Therapy 73

Table of Contents, continued

Chapter 7: Intervention for Pre-linguistic Skills 75
Principles of Pre-linguistic Intervention 75
Attachment 76
Interaction Skills 76
Attention 77
Problem-solving Skills 77
Pragmatics/Communicative Intent 77
Play 79
Long-term and Short-term Goals for Pre-linguistic Behaviors 80
Pre-linguistic Ages of Acquisition/Treatment Objectives 82

Chapter 8: Intervention for Receptive Language 84
Receptive Skills and Cognitive Development 84
Verifying Comprehension 84
Strategies to Develop Receptive Language 85
Long-term and Short-term Goals for Receptive Language 87
Receptive Ages of Acquisition/Treatment Objectives 87

Chapter 9: Intervention for Expressive Language 89
Communicative Intent of the Message 90
Communicative Function Served by the Word Used 92
Semantic-Syntactic Relations 94
Morphemes and Early Sentence Forms 95
Tracking Development of Expressive Language 97
Intervention Techniques to Develop Expressive Language 97
Setting Goals to Develop All Aspects of Expressive Language 99
Expressive Ages of Acquisition/Treatment Objectives 104
Appendix 9A: Tracking Development of Communicative Intent (Pragmatics) 106
Appendix 9B: Relating Core Lexicon to Treatment Objectives 107
Appendix 9C: Development of Communicative Functions 109
Appendix 9D: Tracking Development of Communicative Functions 110
Appendix 9E: Tracking Semantic-Syntactic Relations 111
Appendix 9F: Tracking Development of Morphemes 112
Appendix 9G: Tracking Development of Basic Sentence Types 113
Appendix 9H: New Words 114

Chapter 10: Intervention for Sound Production Development 115
Manual and Touch Cues to Stimulate Sound Production 119
Goals, Treatment Objectives, and Activities for Sound Production Development 122
Sound Production Ages of Acquisition/Treatment Objectives 123

Chapter 11: Augmentative and Alternative Communication 125
Appropriate Populations 125
Types of Augmentative Communication 126
Introducing AAC 130
Speech with Tracheostomy 132
Appendix 11A: Resources 135
Appendix 11B: Suggested Vocabulary Words in Sign Language 137

Table of Contents, *continued*

Chapter 12: Documentation 143
Discipline-Specific Assessment 143
Discipline-Specific Treatment Plan 145
Individualized Family Service Plan (IFSP) 146
Long- and Short-term Goals for Pre-linguistic Skills, Receptive Language Skills,
   Expressive Language Skills, and Sound Production Development 150
Using Progress Notes to Collect Data 154
Six-Month Summary 156
Appendix 12A: Sample Speech & Language Assessment 157
Appendix 12B: Sample Speech-Language Pathology Treatment Plan
              and Discharge Summary 160
Appendix 12C: Sample Individualized Family Service Plan (IFSP) 161
Appendix 12D: Speech and Language Progress Notes (IFSP Meetings) 164
Appendix 12E: Developing Outcomes from Daily Activities 165
Appendix 12F: Selecting Goals, Treatment Objectives, Strategies, and Activities
              to Achieve Parent's Stated Outcome(s) 166
Appendix 12G: Matching Goals and Objectives to Strategies and Activities for the Home .. 167
Appendix 12H: Matching Daily Activities to Treatment Objectives 168
Appendix 12I: Speech and Language Progress Notes 169
Appendix 12J: Sample Six-Month Progress Report 170

References 172

Introduction

There are many unique features about providing services to children birth-to-three years of age. Speech-language pathologists (SLPs) play an integral role in this service provision. The ASHA Position Statement on *The Roles of Speech-Language Pathologists in Service Delivery to Infants, Toddlers, and Their Families* recognizes that SLPs are uniquely qualified to address the broad spectrum of needs of families and their infants and toddlers who are at risk for or who have developmental disabilities. The SLP assumes various roles in addressing these needs, including screening and identification, assessment and evaluation, design, planning, direct service delivery, and monitoring of treatment programs as well as case management and consultation (ASHA 1990). Rossetti (2001) points out that age-appropriate communication is the single best predictor of school performance. "Communication is the developmental domain that with greatest frequency distinguishes at risk from low risk or no risk children" (Rossetti 2001).

Clinical experience with this population is not obtained by most SLPs in graduate school. It is unusual for a graduate clinician to see a child under the age of three, and even more uncommon for them to be given exposure to providing services in a home-based environment. Experienced SLPs trained before the Infants and Toddlers with Disabilities Program, referred to as Part H of The Individuals with Disabilities Education Act (IDEA), was implemented also have limited knowledge about how services to this age group should be provided.

The Early Intervention Kit includes:

- *Therapy Guide*—information on assessment, goals, treatment objectives, treatment methods, augmentative and alternative communication, and documentation

- *Activities Book*—activities for pre-linguistic skills, receptive language, expressive language, and sound production; also parent handouts

- 88 cards with vocabulary words in sign language, including the alphabet and numbers 1-10

The *Therapy Guide* details many of the unique features of providing services to children birth-to-three and provides practical suggestions for dealing with the unique needs of these children and their families. Medical disorders associated with this population are described and efficacy about services to this population is discussed. Approaches to the assessment of communication of young children is also addressed.

Chapters 7–10 (pages 75–124) provide information about treating four main skill areas: pre-linguistic, receptive language, expressive language, and sound production. Chapter 11 (pages 125–142) includes information on the use of augmentative/alternative communication. Chapter 12 (Documentation, pages 143–171) provides examples that should help streamline your paperwork. (Note: Development of feeding/swallowing is not addressed in this kit. *The Source for Pediatric Dysphagia* [Swigert 1998] includes in-depth information on swallowing disorders, feeding techniques, and goals for treatment.)

Introduction, *continued*

Activities for the four main skill areas described in Chapters 7-10 are in the *Activities Book*. These activities can be completed in therapy and can be demonstrated to caregivers to help infants and toddlers achieve short-term goals in these areas. Parent handouts are also found in the *Activities Book*. These handouts include a variety of information for parents (e.g., language development, strategies to facilitate communication).

Many children in the birth-to-three age range with delayed expressive language are exposed to the use of manual signs to augment their communication attempts and to stimulate their verbal language development. The cards in this kit have pictures and descriptions of 88 manual signs that can serve as a resource in therapy or that can be copied for caregivers.

The Early Intervention Kit is not intended to be a curriculum but rather a compilation of information and activities you can use to implement a treatment plan. You have the flexibility to choose the goals to address and the treatment activities to address those goals. After identifying the child's and family's needs, an individualized treatment plan can be developed using the included long-term and short-term goals. Then you can choose the treatment objectives/activities to help the child achieve those goals.

This kit has truly been a team effort on the part of the staff of Swigert & Associates, Inc. Some of my associates have written chapters in the *Therapy Guide* and others have contributed significantly to the development of the activities in the *Activities Book*. All of the contributors are seasoned providers of early intervention services, recognizable by the trunks full of toys in their vehicles, briefcases full of charts with detailed notes and reports, and broad smiles on their faces from the delight of making a difference in a young child's life.

We hope the information in this kit will make service provision easier for you, and leave you with a smile on your face.

Nancy	Kim
Jennifer	Michelle
Sarah S.	Ashley
Verity	Lissa
Sarah C.	Julie

Chapter 1

The Evolution of Early Intervention

Early childhood special education received a significant boost in 1986 when PL 99-457 amended PL 94-142 by extending the full-service mandate to preschoolers and establishing a new program for infants, toddlers, and their families (Part H). This legislation represented the culmination of nearly 25 years of federal legislation related to early childhood special education. (In 1990, the title of *Education of the Handicapped Act* was changed to the *Individuals with Disabilities Education Act* (IDEA). The Infants and Toddlers with Disabilities Program, which had been referred to as Part H, became subchapter VIII [though it is still commonly referred to as Part H].) The Part H component of the law is voluntary.

In 1986, Part H funding created a discretionary program to assist states in planning, developing, and implementing a statewide system of comprehensive, multidisciplinary interagency services for all young children with disabilities ages birth to three. States could apply for incentive grants to help support the development of statewide systems for services. All states chose to apply for such funds.

Before the enactment of Part H funding, speech-language pathologists (SLPs) had few opportunities to provide services to children under the age of three. Specialized preschool settings typically did not enroll children younger than three (and typically not before they were toilet trained). Many pediatricians did not think about referring a toddler for speech-language services. The thought process may have been that "children that age don't talk enough to need therapy." Infants and toddlers who were referred through existing programs like home health were usually those who had severe impairments. Children with mild development delays were usually kept in a "wait and see" mode. Infants and toddlers at risk were often not even identified as at risk.

When states organized and implemented their early intervention programs, SLPs found themselves faced with serving children much younger than those with whom they had gained experience. They also found that the therapy methods/models they had used with older children did not work well with infants and toddlers. SLPs were not alone. The field of early intervention evolved as all disciplines gained knowledge and skills with this population and began to change how they provided services.

Traditional Curriculum Models

Noonan and McCormick (1993) summarize three traditional curriculum models for service delivery that highlight this evolution:

- *Developmental Curriculum Model*—Considered the original early intervention curriculum model, and sometimes referred to as an *enrichment model*. The goal of the developmental model is to assist infants and young children with disabilities to progress through the normal sequence of development. The activities provide opportunities for demonstrating and encouraging the milestones that are being targeted.

- *Developmental-Cognitive Model*—This model is based on the work of Jean Piaget (1926, 1970). Cognitive skills are emphasized, and the theory concludes that cognitive development occurs as a result of the child's growth and interaction with the environment. The tasks presented are challenging so that the child will learn how to solve the challenge.

- *Behavioral Model*—Based on learning principles of behavioral psychologists such as B. F. Skinner, it describes development and learning as resulting from environmental interactions. Direct instruction involves prompting, shaping, and reinforcing in a consistent fashion.

Shift toward naturalistic focus

All three of these models have evolved toward a more naturalistic focus for early intervention. The developmentalists have changed their focus to include an emphasis on child/caregiver interaction. Behaviors are interpreted in the context of the interaction with the caregiver. Each behavior is viewed as part of the cycle.

The developmental-cognitive model now includes a strong social development component based largely on the work of Bruner (1975, 1977) who describes early social skills as "social-cognitive" behaviors that serve a pre-linguistic function. This model also recognizes the relationship of these behaviors to environmental control. The infant learns that his behavior can change the environment.

The behavioral model shifted to a naturalistic perspective in the way goals were selected and instructional procedures were chosen. The goals now relate to environmental demands and expectations. Skills are no longer taught in isolation, but are taught in sequence with other skills that would naturally occur. In addition, the focus is on generalizing skills rather than teaching a specific skill. For instance, if the child is learning to gesture for "more," he is not taught to do this just in the context of asking for more food, but he is taught this skill in many contexts.

Naturalistic Model

In a naturalistic model, the emphasis is for services to be provided in a naturalistic or natural environment. This typically means the child's home or child-care setting, as opposed to a clinical or office setting. These natural environments offer a wide variety of opportunities for language development. The dog barking next door, the garbage truck rumbling down the street, the sibling refusing to share a toy are all realistic situations a child may encounter. What could be more perfect for stimulating language? For example, it's much more effective to teach the child to say "shh" to the barking dog than to try to stimulate that utterance in a clinical setting.

A naturalistic environment is just one part of providing services in a naturalistic model. Using a naturalistic model also involves:

- Making sure the treatment plan and activities meet the unique needs and lifestyles of the child, family, peers, and community.

- Planning instruction that can be implemented naturally in daily routines of the family.

- Emphasizing skills that are functional for the child both now and in the future (McDonnell & Hardman 1988).

It is clear how each of the components can be more easily achieved if the services are provided in the child's natural environment. In the natural environment, the lifestyle of the family is more obvious. You see the child and his family engaged in the activities of their daily lives. You see which routines take place on a day-to-day basis so that you can suggest ways the caregivers can implement the treatment plan during those routines. You can also see how the child can apply the skills taught and therefore, can choose skills that are particularly important to this child in his environment.

The way that goals and treatment objectives are selected is also different in a naturalistic model when compared to a developmental-curriculum or developmental-cognitive model. In the latter two models, the goals and treatment objectives are chosen by comparing the child to a developmental skill sequence. Instruction then begins on skills the child is unable to complete in the normal sequence of development. In a naturalistic model, goals and treatment objectives are chosen by identifying and analyzing the routines and activities that occur in the natural environment. The naturalistic model, of course, includes goals that would appear on a developmental list, but they may be selected earlier if needed in a routine or activity.

Choosing goals based on a developmental list is most appropriate for children who are at risk for delay or who have a mild delay or disability. This is the majority of children served in most early intervention programs. Choosing goals based on a developmental model may not be as appropriate for children with severe multiple disabilities. These children may not be able to achieve certain milestones because of their disabilities. Adaptations to the skills will need to be made.

One of the most important features of a naturalistic model is the opportunities provided to the child to generalize skills learned. The skills are not taught in a therapeutic situation, but rather in activities that naturally occur in the child's environment. The child is given multiple opportunities to practice the skill in a variety of activities that occur on a daily basis. Remember that the child may be in many environments throughout the day, including his home, child-care situation, a relative's home, playground, yard, and/or a friend's home. Activities should be selected that might occur in any or all of those environments.

The naturalistic environment also provides the best opportunity for caregiver training. The ultimate goal of early intervention is for the child to achieve developmental milestones, just as this is the goal for older children. However, with older children this is mostly accomplished by direct work with the child. In the birth-to-three population, the role of the interventionist is to teach the caregivers how to help the child achieve the milestones. The therapist serves as a teacher, model, and consultant more so than as a direct service provider.

Chapter 2

Unique Features of Service Delivery

Some aspects of providing services to children birth to three may be totally different than when working with older children (e.g., providing services in the home), while other features may be important when working with any age child (e.g., behavior management techniques). These features might be grouped into the following major categories:

- Service Delivery Model (pages 14–20)

- Child Characteristics and Needs (pages 20–23)

- Treatment Planning (pages 23–24)

- Treatment Methods (See Chapter 6, pages 66–72.)

- Treatment Materials (See Chapter 6, pages 72–74.)

- Documentation (See Chapter 12, pages 143–171.)

Service Delivery Model: Considerations and Modifications

Providing services in the natural environment

The benefits of providing services in a natural environment are many. Hanft and Pilkington (2000) indicate key benefits for the child, family, and therapists:

- enhanced relationships among family members (including siblings), therapists, and caregivers

- ability to model for and assist caregivers as they help improve the child's performance

- improved capacity to assess the child's strengths and select meaningful outcomes

- improved ability to analyze family dynamics

If providing services at the child's daycare center, meet with the teacher and classroom aide to explain the services you will be providing. Discuss the ways you can take advantage of this natural environment. Can other children from the class be engaged in the activities? Children who are already exhibiting the skill you are trying to develop can serve as wonderful role models. The child may also be more willing to participate when she sees her classmates participating.

Making home visits can be challenging and some ground rules should be established at the beginning of intervention.

1. It is critical for the caregiver to understand how important it is for the child to be able to pay attention to and participate in the activities. Therapy should be scheduled at the time of day when the child is most alert and has been fed.

2. Discuss that you will want the caregivers involved in the sessions. If this is not made clear, parents may view your visit as a chance to get caught up on things around the home.

3. Ask if there are particular times of day when the home is a little quieter (e.g. when the older siblings are in school) and/or if there is a place in the home that might be less distracting to the child. If the only room in which you can see the child is the room with the television, ask if the television can be turned off during your visit. You may have to help the caregiver understand the kind of learning environment you are trying to foster.

If these ground rules are discussed during the first session, the caregiver will be more likely to provide this modified environment each time you make a home visit.

Begin each home visit by allowing the caregivers to fill you in on things that have happened since your last visit. Ask if the child has demonstrated any change in skills. Inquire whether the specific strategies and activities suggested during the last visit were helpful. If the child is seen at daycare, the teacher should be able to supply this information. When the child is seen at daycare, an extra effort needs to be made to communicate with the parents since they probably will not be at the daycare during your visit.

Some infants and children in need of early intervention services are from low-income families. Some of the homes you visit may lack stimulating toys and books, and the families may not have the means to purchase such items. In addition, some homes may not be as clean as is desired for a toddler crawling around on the floor. Wear comfortable, washable clothes on the days home services are provided. Another helpful strategy is to take along a plastic or vinyl tablecloth. This serves several purposes. It defines an area in which you want the child to stay by providing a clear boundary for the "work" area and gives you and the child a clean surface on which to sit.

In some instances, home visits will be made in high crime areas. You should place personal safety as the most important goal. If a situation ever presents itself in which you do not feel safe, leave the home immediately and contact the agency sponsoring the visit for advice on how to proceed.

You may also encounter families who frequently are not at home for the regularly scheduled visit. To avoid this, you may want to call each family the morning of the visit to remind them of the scheduled appointment. If you arrive at the home and the family is not there, leaving a note on the door is a good reminder to the family that they missed an appointment.

> Date _____ Time _____
>
> Sorry I missed you. I arrived on time for our scheduled visit but no one was home.
>
> ____ Please call me to reschedule.
>
> ____ Please be home at _____ on _____ for our next visit.
>
> _____
> Speech-Language Pathologist

Serving in a consultative role

When providing services to children birth to three, you will serve more as consultant than as a direct service provider. You may visit the child in her home once a week or perhaps once every several weeks. LeLaurin (1992) summarizes how important the consultative role is. She indicates that if the only intervention the child received was for the hour a week the professional was with the child, this would represent approximately 1% of the child's annual waking time. Obviously for intervention to be effective, it must occur throughout the child's day. That means that the caregiver has to be the primary interventionist.

The main purpose of your visit is to serve as a consultant to the caregivers. A consultative process can be seen as a problem-solving process (Coleman et al. 1995). The problems are those areas in which the child is not demonstrating adequate communication and/or feeding/swallowing development. At each visit, discuss the child's progress and analyze how well the child has responded to the strategies the caregiver has implemented since you last visited. Establish the next step for the child. Work with the caregiver to identify strategies she can use to help the child continue to develop. In a consultative role, you utilize listening skills and interview skills to help you analyze the problem, evaluate the problem, and implement a plan.

Greater involvement of caregivers

Although involving caregivers in a client's treatment is always important, it is **crucial** with this age child. Without the support and involvement of the caregivers, treatment will be much less successful. In fact, the current focus is for the family to be considered the unit of intervention rather than the child. This recognizes that the family system is a complex and interdependent one and that supporting that system is the best way to have a positive impact on the child (Hershberger 1991).

Having a child with special needs has a significant impact on family dynamics. It may limit the family's ability to fulfill typical functions. There may be family circumstances that interfere with the caregiver's ability to deal with the child in the most appropriate way. Hershberger stresses the importance of being sensitive to the fact that family members may be grieving for the child they thought they were going to have, and adjusting to the child they do have.

The most important goal of any therapy for a child in the birth-to-three age range is for you to teach the caregivers how to teach the child. This does not mean that you are trying to turn every caregiver into a SLP. It does mean, however, that you need to explain to the caregivers the rationale for what you're doing. You also need to teach caregivers how to do what you're doing so they can continue to practice with the child on a daily basis.

Caregivers have varying levels of knowledge about early childhood development and various levels of expertise for implementing home programs. Caregivers may also present with different learning styles. Some may be able to watch the session and, with no further explanation, think of five different ways that they can work on the same treatment objectives throughout the week. Others respond well to written material explaining what you expect them to do. Still others need to actually try the activity while you make suggestions to them about ways to improve the activity. Do not assume that by watching what you do, the caregiver will be able to do it.

Although it is sometimes awkward to assume the role of teacher for another adult, it is often a good idea to demonstrate an activity with the child while the caregiver watches. Then ask the caregiver to repeat the activity while you watch and offer suggestions.

In order for a skill to become established, the child will have to practice it often. Families are very busy, and even those with the best intentions will find it difficult to set aside specific time to work on a communication or swallowing activity. In order for the child to be given ample opportunity to practice skill development, the caregiver needs to be shown how to use simple activities of daily living to accomplish this practice. Parent handouts in the *Activities Book* (pages 159–162 and 164–185) are designed to help you show the caregivers how to use the natural environment for learning.

The Individualized Family Service Plan (IFSP) process

The increased involvement of the caregiver is very apparent in the IFSP process. If you work with older children, then you are used to a model in which you test the child and then share the results with the parents, including your recommendations for treatment. The IEP process for school-age children involves the family but not to the same extent as in the IFSP process. With the IFSP, your role is as a collaborator and a partner with the family. The family is viewed as an active member of the team (Bender & Baglin 1992).

The plan is developed jointly with the caregivers and all of the specialists involved in providing care to the child. Bender and Baglin summarize this nicely when they state, "Thus, the IFSP *process* assumes greater significance than the resulting *document*, which should serve primarily as a written reflection of the information exchange between families and professionals, and subsequent decision-making by families."

What are some differences you might notice in IFSP meetings? The members of the team will listen carefully to what caregivers have to say about the child's strengths and weaknesses, and about what they would like the child to be able to do. They often ask open-ended questions to elicit more information.

You will be asked to suggest specific strategies and activities the caregivers can use in the home to help achieve the goals listed for communication and swallowing.* The process is not concerned with the methodologies you'll use as the clinician: it is concerned with how the caregiver will be able to incorporate these activities into daily living.

> The functions of open-ended questions:
>
> 1. Invite comments from family members without limiting what they want to express.
>
> 2. Encourage family members to elaborate on a point.
>
> 3. Help describe an action or behavior more specifically.
>
> 4. Focus and clarify family members' actions and priorities.

Performing an evaluation vs. an assessment

One of the idiosyncrasies of the early intervention system is the use of the terms *evaluation* and *assessment*. An *evaluation* is the first testing the child undergoes to determine if she qualifies for services. This evaluation will cover all areas of development (e.g., cognitive, fine motor, gross motor, communication). Based on the results of this evaluation, the child may be referred to other specialists (e.g., physical therapist, SLP, audiologist) for an *assessment* that will determine the child's needs, and the strengths and needs of the family. The assessment forms the basis for the intervention services.

Working with a case manager

An important part of the framework for providing services to infants and children is the use of case management. The case manager is responsible for helping the family obtain the needed services, making sure the services are delivered in a timely way and coordinating the provision of the services. The case manager coordinates the different assessments the child needs (e.g., speech-language pathology, physical therapy, developmental intervention), helps the family identify available service providers, guides the development of the IFSP, coordinates and monitors the delivery of services, and coordinates care with medical and health providers (Gilbert et al. 1992). In early intervention, the case manager is usually called a service coordinator.

Working as part of a team

Many children under the age of three who qualify for early intervention services will receive intervention by more than one discipline. It is important that the different professionals working with the child and family closely coordinate their services. This coordination will make it easier for the family to use the strategies for achieving the child's goals. For example, physical therapy (PT) may have a goal for the child to be able to get down safely from the couch and the SLP may have a goal to increase single word utterances. By collaborating, the physical

---

*Development of feeding/swallowing is not addressed in this kit. See *The Source for Pediatric Dysphagia* (Swigert 1998).

therapist and the SLP can ask the caregiver to use this one activity (getting down from the couch) to work on the physical goal as well as to use the word *down* each time, thus improving the child's language skills.

There are different types of team models that may be utilized. A *multi-disciplinary* approach is one in which individual team members retain their distinctive roles, but exchange information about what each is doing. An *interdisciplinary* model is more cooperative. Team members make an effort to incorporate information and techniques they have learned from other disciplines into their treatment. For example, the SLP might utilize information learned from the PT about positioning when working with the child. The *transdisciplinary* model makes a conscious effort to take on some of the roles of another discipline.

Hershberger (1991) describes steps team members take toward achieving a transdisciplinary model.

> *Role extension* is a process through which team members keep abreast of the latest developments in their field. For example, the SLP attends yearly early intervention conferences and reads journal articles on the topic.
>
> *Role enrichment* is a general awareness and understanding of other disciplines and a sharing of information about basic practices. For example, the occupational therapist (OT) shares information with the SLP about what types of toys might cause sensory overload for the child. The SLP might share information with the physical therapist (PT) about how to stimulate the use of action words during physical therapy.
>
> *Role expansion* involves exchanging information on how to make some judgments outside your discipline. The SLP might train other therapists about expected ages of acquisition of communication skills so the other therapists know when a referral is needed.
>
> *Role exchange* involves working side-by-side to acquire skills outside your discipline to incorporate into your work with the child. For example, the PT might show you how to perform exercises to improve the child's balance and the SLP might show the PT how to teach production of sounds.

Coordinating services with other agencies

The family can choose the service providers that they want to work with their child. They may choose therapists from different agencies. If this is the case, then each therapist (e.g., PT, SLP, OT, developmental interventionist) has to extend extra effort to regularly talk with the other professionals on the team.

Transitioning to the next level of care—the preschool environment

A *transition* is defined as a point of change in services and in the personnel who provide these services. When children reach the age of three, they are no longer eligible for early intervention services under the Federal Part H funding. It can be a stressful time for families to change practitioners and settings. The services may have been provided in the home or at the child's daycare until the age of three, but most likely at three years of age the child will have to go to the school to receive continued services. The case manager will facilitate this transition. Usually this will include a meeting of all the professionals who have been treating the child as well as representatives from agencies who will treat the child after the transition. Noonan and McCormick (1993) describe eleven skills from the *Preschool Preparation and Transition Program* in Hawaii as being particularly important for a child to successfully participate in a classroom environment. When working with children nearing the age of three, keep in mind that these are important skills to target to ease the transition to a preschool setting:

- follows general rules and routines
- expresses wants and needs
- cooperates with/helps others
- complies with directions given by adult
- shares materials/toys with peers
- socializes with peers
- takes turns
- interacts verbally with adults
- interacts verbally with peers
- focuses attention on the speaker
- makes own decisions

The assessment checklists and skill definitions of all 27 skills from the Hawaii project are reprinted in Appendix 2A, pages 25–28.

Child Characteristics and Needs

Johnson-Martin et al. (1991) describe some of the features that are important to keep in mind when working with this population. Those and others are summarized here and in Chapter 6 (*Treatment Methods, Techniques, and Materials*, pages 66–74).

The child needs choices

An important part of developing a sense of some control for a child is being able to make choices. Even young infants can make a choice about what they look at, or whether or not they will continue to take their bottles. Being offered choices is also an important lesson for the child in early communication. If you take several toys into the treatment session, you might hold up two and let the child select which she wants to play with first. Only offer choices where either "answer" is acceptable.

The child needs routine to provide security

Young children appreciate routine. They like knowing what to expect in certain situations and from certain people. Using this principle in your treatment sessions may gain more cooperation from the child. This may be something as simple as always working in the same location, always finishing the session with the same reinforcement (e.g., sticker, cookie, hug good-bye), or completing similar activities in the same order each session. For instance, you might always begin the session with a gross motor activity to accomplish direction following for the child who has trouble settling into an activity that requires more specific attention. This might be followed with an activity in which the child is expected to sit and pay careful attention to a picture book for the next few minutes. Another child might prefer the routine to begin with an activity during which her mother holds her before you introduce an activity in which she is expected to get down from her mother's lap and play on the floor.

The child from a culturally diverse background

In any setting, and with all clients, it is important to be sensitive to the cultural needs of the client being served. What makes it more important when serving this population is that you are often providing service in the client's home. Being culturally sensitive requires you to learn about the different cultures and child-rearing techniques of the families you serve. You must also examine your own cultural values and beliefs to determine the influence they have had on how you interact with children (Chang & Pulido 1994).

Anderson & McNeilly (1992) provide a thorough discussion about the issues involved in meeting the needs of children and families from culturally diverse backgrounds. They give examples of some cross-cultural value differences from the typical Anglo-American view that may be encountered:

- Fatalism vs. personal control
  Many families from ethno-linguistically diverse populations may have a fatalistic outlook concerning the child's disability with a sense of personal responsibility for the care of the young child. That means the family may turn to other family and friends for support before seeking help from professionals.

- Orientation to the past instead of the future
  Instead of looking forward and recognizing the importance of early intervention for the child's future, the family may view following traditional practices and customs as most important. This view may be tied closely to viewing the disability as God's will, or punishment for past deeds.

- Hierarchy, rank, and status vs. human equality
  An equalitarian view allows family members to see themselves on equal footing with the professionals serving the child. Families from culturally diverse backgrounds may defer to a hierarchy within the family or defer to the professional.

Anderson & McNeilly point out that there is a "dynamic interaction between a family's cultural beliefs, values, experiences, and expectations, child-rearing and management practices, and the young child's development." Because of that, it is important for professionals working with the child and family to gain an understanding and awareness of cultural diversity.

Making adaptations for children with physical limitations

When providing therapy to a child with physical limitations, you may have to make adaptations in the treatment objectives and in the activities you will use to achieve those objectives. Ask the caregivers for information about the child's limitations and for strategies they have used to help the child deal with the limitations.

For a child with a *visual impairment*, remember to:

- minimize the interference of glare and shadows

- maximize desirable light

- tell the child you're going to touch her before you do, so as not to startle her

- remind the child to use speech/words, as the child with a visual impairment may not see the direct association between her words and subsequent action of others

- describe objects to the child and help her use her hands to explore the objects

For a child with a *hearing impairment*, remember to:

- call the child's name when addressing her and wait until you have her attention

- sit in a well-lit area so the child can see your face

- use gestures and pointing to supplement your speech

- use facial expressions when talking

For the child with a *motor/movement impairment*, remember to:

- adapt the treatment objective to account for the limitation (e.g., if the objective is for the child to imitate gestures with adults but the child cannot use her upper extremities, you might change the objective to imitation of movement of the head such as a head nod or shake)

- learn how to position and move the child by consulting with the physical therapist, occupational therapist, and/or caregiver

- learn what special adaptive equipment the child uses for sitting, standing, and floor activities

- select toys and materials that might be more easily operated by the child (e.g., puzzles with large wooden knobs on the pieces or a windup toy with large crank)

Treatment Planning

The assessment may yield many more goals than can be addressed at one time. The team, with the caregivers as an integral part, reviews the needs and potential goals identified by each discipline. The family helps narrow the list and prioritize timing by identifying their greatest concerns for the child. If there is a difference of opinion between the professionals and the parents about the child's greatest needs, the professionals can express their views and explain why they think a certain need is most important for the child, but they must ultimately yield to the family's wishes.

Hanft and Pilkington (2000) list several questions that can be answered by the team to help in selecting goals:

1. What does the child need to learn or do next? What is the outcome the caregivers would like to achieve? Some families may have trouble selecting priorities for their child. Helpful questions are provided by Noonan and McCormick (1993) to help the family establish priorities:

    - If we could only write one goal, what would it be?

    - If your child could pick one skill to learn, what do you think she would pick?

    - Are there skills that would enable your child to participate in family activities?

    - Are there skills that would make your home life easier?

    - Are there skills your child has almost learned?

    - Are there skills that would greatly increase the number of activities your child can participate in?

2. Which intervention strategies and natural environments will facilitate the child's specific developmental outcome? Although treatment planning for the child birth to three mirrors treatment planning for older children in many ways, the development of strategies is unique. These are some ways that treatment planning is the same (along with some subtle differences) across populations:

    - identifies areas of deficit (in birth-to-three population they are called *needs*) as well as strengths to build on

    - establishes long-term and short-term goals (but with much more parent input)

    - determines treatment objectives that will be used to reach those goals

Chapter 2: Unique Features of Service Delivery

With this birth-to-three population, you also have to determine specific strategies the caregivers can use to work on the treatment objectives and suggest activities that might be conducive to specific treatment objectives. An explanation of strategies is included as a parent handout in the *Activities Book*, pages 159–161. Refer to these strategies when participating in the development of the IFSP. Examples of activities for Chapter 7–10 can also be found in the *Activities Book* on pages 10–42, 45–72, 78–120, 124–150, 162, and 164–185.

3. Whose experience is needed to help a child achieve the desired outcomes? Which professionals need to be involved to help maximize the child's development?

4. How and where should services be provided? Does the specific goal lend itself to direct intervention by the therapist, a combination of work by the therapist and carryover by the parents, or primary intervention provided by the parents with the therapist(s) serving in a consultative role? Should the services be provided in the home or day care?

Summary

The unique features of providing services to children between birth and three years of age and their families make this an exciting population with which to work. However, if you are used to providing services to older children, you must make significant adjustments in order to be successful with this population.

Appendix 2A

Hawaii Preparing for Integrated Preschool (PIP) Assessment
Preschool Preparation and Transition Project   University of Hawaii at Manoa

IS THE SKILL MASTERED?
+ Yes   **/** Partially
− No
0 No Opportunity to Observe

Child's Name: _____ Date of Birth: _____

Assessor: _____

		Date Skill Mastered	Comments
Self-Help	1. Grasps objects		
	2. Drinks independently		
	3. Eats independently		
	4. Cares for toileting needs		
	5. Cares for personal hygiene		
	6. Moves about independently		
Classroom Routines	7. Makes transitions from one activity to another		
	8. Complies with directions		
	9. Follows rules and routines		
	10. Knows and recognizes name		
	11. Focuses on task		
	12. Uses materials appropriately		
	13. Throws rubbish in wastebasket		
	14. Puts materials away when finished		
Communication/Socialization	15. Focuses attention on speaker		
	16. Expresses wants/needs		
	17. Socializes with others		
	18. Problem-solves with words		
	19. Makes own decisions		
	20. Communicates with peers		
	21. Communicates with adults		
	22. Takes turns		
	23. Shares materials/toys with peers		
	24. Responds when spoken to		
	25. Cooperates with/helps others		
	26. Does not disturb peers		
	27. Uses voice appropriate to activity		

Adapted and reprinted from *Early Intervention in Natural Environments: Methods & Procedures*, 1st Edition by Noonan & McCormick. ©1993. Reprinted with permission of Delmar Learning, a division of Thomson Learning. www.thomsonrights.com. Fax 800-730-2215.

continued on next page

Appendix 2A

Hawaii Preparing for Integrated Preschool (PIP) Skill Definitions

	Skill	*Definition*
Self-Help	1. Grasps objects	Child grasps and holds objects such as fat pencils, crayons, manipulative toys, and other small objects (typical response of 3-year-old; without assistance)
	2. Drinks independently	Given a cup, juice box, or thermos, child picks up cup, juice box, or thermos and sips from cup, straw, or thermos spout without assistance (typical response of 3-year-old; without assistance)
	3. Eats independently	During snack or lunch, child completes meal within 30 minutes, feeding himself finger foods with his hands and other foods with a spoon and a fork (typical response of 3-year-old; without assistance)
	4. Cares for toileting needs	Child performs all aspects of toileting independently, communicating need to go to the bathroom, independence in managing clothing, toileting, washing/drying hands. Some assistance with clothing fasteners may be required (typical response of 3-year-old; independently)
	5. Cares for personal hygiene	Child covers nose or mouth when sneezing/coughing when reminded by an adult; washes hands, cleans face, and wipes nose at routine times (e.g., before/after snack, cooking, outdoor play) (typical response of 3-year-old; long duration, independently)
	6. Moves about independently	Child moves independently either walking or with the use of adaptive aids (e.g., wheelchair, scooterboard, walker) (typical response of 3-year-old; long duration, independently)
Classroom Routines	7. Makes transitions from one activity to another	At transition points between any activities, child responds to a familiar signal. Child's response includes completion of one activity and movement to area for next activity within the allotted time (typical response of 3-year-old; with one announcement)
	8. Complies with directions	Child complies to teacher's verbal request to perform routine activities or change behavior (typical response of 3-year-old; immediately)
	9. Follows rules and routines	Child complies to teacher's verbal request, participates with group, and adheres to safety rules (typical response of 3-year-old; with one verbal reminder)

continued on next page

	Skill	Definition
Classroom Routines	10. Knows and recognizes name	In classroom areas (e.g., on cubby) or during activities (e.g., circle), child recognizes his/her printed name by finding correct flash card or labeled cubby (typical response of 3-year-old; first and last name without prompts)
	11. Focuses on task	Child attends to any activity that requires concentration (e.g., story time, art, or music) until task is complete. Child appears "tuned into task," sitting, gazing, manipulating, and performing task (typical response of 3-year-old; looks, manipulates, performs more than once)
	12. Uses materials appropriately	Child manipulates toys, art supplies, games, blocks, and/or outdoor equipment in manner that each is intended to be used (typical response of 3-year-old; without reminder)
	13. Throws rubbish in wastebasket	After any activity that creates rubbish, child picks up all rubbish, takes it to wastebasket, and places it in wastebasket (typical response of 3-year-old; without reminder)
	14. Puts materials away when finished	At the signaled end of an activity, child places classroom materials, personal belongings, and rubbish in the correct places (typical response of 3-year-old; with one verbal reminder)
Communication/Socialization	15. Focuses attention on speaker	When one adult talks to child or group of children, child listens attentively: looking at speaker, sitting or standing quietly, and not interrupting, for an appropriate length of time (typical response of 3-year-old; not interrupting, quiet, looks at speaker intermittently)
	16. Expresses wants/needs	When a child wants or needs something such as a toy or a drink of water, the child asks for it (typical response of 3-year-old; verbally)
	17. Socializes with others	Child solicits attention of another child or responds to a child's bid for attention either positively or negatively (typical response of 3-year-old; talks)
	18. Problem-solves with words	In a situation involving physical or verbal conflict, child uses words to resolve the conflict so that play either continues or ends (typical response of 3-year-old; independently)
	19. Makes own decisions	Child chooses materials/activity, location, or person when a choice is presented (typical response of 3-year-old; immediately)

continued on next page

Appendix 2A

	Skill	Definition
Communication/Socialization	20. Communicates with peers	Child initiates or responds, either verbally or through alternative means (e.g., sign language, communication board), to peer about different topics (typical response of 3-year-old; single turns)
	21. Communicates with adults	Child initiates or responds, either verbally or through alternative means (e.g., sign language, communication board), to adults about different topics (typical response of 3-year-old; single turns)
	22. Takes turns	In group activities that require taking turns (e.g., using outdoor equipment, playing circle games) child waits without protest for his/her turn, participates, and gives up his/her turn without protest (typical response of 3-year-old; with one or no reminders)
	23. Shares materials/toys with peers	When two children are playing with same materials, child releases material to another child even briefly (typical response of 3-year-old; independently)
	24. Responds when spoken to	When individually addressed by adult or peer throughout the day, child shifts attention to speaker: turning toward, looking at, talking to, or stopping ongoing activity (typical response of 3-year-old; immediately)
	25. Cooperates with/helps others	When engaged in an activity, child participates without protest or struggle, or offers help to another person (typical response of 3-year-old; independently)
	26. Does not disturb peers	Child does not use hands or feet to distract or hurt another child, refrains from making loud or inappropriate noises, and does not talk out of turn (typical response of 3-year-old; independently)
	27. Uses voice appropriate to activity	When engaged in indoor activity, child talks in conversational tones. When requested to use softer/louder volume, child responds accordingly (typical response of 3-year-old; without reminder)

Therapy Guide
The Early Intervention Kit

Chapter 3

Evidence Base for Early Intervention

Research in the area of early intervention has been divided into two broad categories delineated by the passage of PL 99-457. Guralnick (1993, 1997) dubs these categories as first generation and second generation research, and indicates that the first generation of research conducted prior to the passage of PL 99-457 demonstrated "general effectiveness and feasibility of early intervention programs for children born at risk as well as for those with established disabilities" and for providing the context for evaluating systems approaches, curricula, and specific techniques. Many have recognized the limitations of the first generation of research in this area, indicating that it did not address the complexities of providing early intervention services, nor did it address the recognition of more populations of children who are at risk for delay.

Guralnick indicates that the second generation of research must help to determine the interventions that work best for which children and under what conditions. In particular, more research in the second generation should focus on the influence of child and family characteristics on the outcomes of the intervention. Guralnick also indicates that second generation research should focus on research on two groups of children: those with established disabilities and those at-risk. For a comprehensive look at a review of first generation research and an agenda for the second generation research, readers are referred to *The Effectiveness of Early Intervention* (Guralnick 1997).

The area of early intervention faces specific challenges in conducting research to demonstrate the efficacy of this intervention. Baer (1981) calls these challenges the "sociological impossibilities" of being able to identify and study all the components present in the intervention program. There is also the challenge of trying to compare the different intervention approaches used in early intervention. Bricker and Cripe (1992) point out that research in this area is improving. In addition to evaluating intervention approaches from the perspective of child change, the research is also focusing on the effect the intervention has on the family dynamics, and on whether the caregiver can effectively implement the strategies.

Effectiveness of Early Intervention

Bennett (1995) summarizes the results of one comprehensive long-term controlled investigation that studied the effectiveness of developmental interventions for biologically-vulnerable infants and toddlers provided through the local Infant Health and Development Program. These children received home visits throughout the first three years of life, attendance at a full day child development center between ages one and three, transportation, and periodic checkups. The parents were involved in parent education group meetings. The group that received intervention performed better on intelligence tests and the mothers reported fewer behavior problems.

Other studies demonstrate the effectiveness of home visiting:

- Both inner-city and rural children who received home-based early intervention showed significantly better cognitive development than children who did not receive such services (Bryant & Ramey 1987).

- Home visiting was found to be more effective if it was begun early after discharge from hospital. It also appeared to be more effective if there were one primary visitor making frequent visits (Heincke et al. 1989).

- Children who were developmentally delayed showed increased social conversational skills when they received home visiting intervention (Girolometto 1988).

- Fewer additional services were needed by low birthweight children who had completed a two-year program of home visiting when compared to children who did not receive services (Grantham-McGregor 1987).

A study by Warfield (1995) demonstrates the complexity of trying to determine cost-effectiveness of home visiting versus group services. The study attempted to analyze the amount of change in adaptive behavior, mother-child interaction, and parenting stress. The results indicate that the outcomes varied by subgroup and also by the outcome measure. For example, the reduction in parenting stress was larger for those who received one hour of home visiting compared to those who received one hour of group services. For the younger children, the largest changes per hour on both mother-child interaction and parenting stress were associated with group services on both interaction measures.

McWilliam (1996) reviewed published and unpublished research on integrated versus pull-out service delivery models and concluded that although integrated therapy had only marginally-better effects than segregated services on skill acquisition and generalization, it had positive effects on collaboration.

Effectiveness of Types of Intervention

Bricker and Cripe (1992) analyzed intervention research and categorized the research as either an adult-directed approach or a child-directed approach. Some of the studies analyzed by these authors are summarized below.

Giumento (1990) reviewed six intervention studies and concluded:

- Well-defined approaches produce change in children regardless of the orientation of the approach.

- Didactic approaches produce greater gains in acquisition of specific skills.

- Child-directed approaches produce better problem-solving skills.

Cole et al. (1991) found that:

- Relatively higher-performing students gained more from direct instruction.

- Relatively lower-performing students gained more from mediated learning.

The findings by Giumento and Cole et al. were similar to those in a study by Yoder et al. (1991). Bricker and Cripe point out that this support of child-directed approaches is contrary to the belief that children with more significant impairments need a more structured, adult-directed approach.

Bricker and colleagues (1981, 1982, 1988) have published many articles analyzing the effectiveness of their activity-based interaction. Their approach is based on the work of Vygotsky (1978). The goal of activity-based interaction is to improve children's acquisition and use of important skills integrated into functional, child-initiated, social activities. They point out weaknesses in these studies that are common with most outcomes studies: that the studies were completed without controls and that the functional change seen in children cannot be directly attributed to the program because of many other factors (e.g., growth, parent involvement). Nonetheless, these four studies (Bricker and colleagues) support the use of activity-based intervention as the children showed gains on norm-referenced and criterion-referenced tools.

Findings on Child Outcomes vs. Family Outcomes

Bailey et al. (1998) indicate that most evaluations of effectiveness of early intervention focus on outcomes for children. However, the focus for early intervention has broadened to a family focus (also called *family-centered*, *family-friendly*, or *family-directed*). This focus recognizes the responsibility to support families of children with disabilities. Part H asserted that a major goal of early intervention is to "enhance the capacity of families to meet the special needs of their infants and toddlers with disabilities" (Education of the Handicapped Act Amendments of 1986, Public Law 99-457*). Bailey et al. indicate two broad areas that might be assessed: family perception of the early intervention experience and impact on the family.

Most parents report a high degree of satisfaction with early intervention services, though most of these studies are completed with parent satisfaction questionnaires (McNaughton 1994). One inherent weakness in this approach is that parents have no standard against which to judge the services they received (Simeonsson 1988). Families may feel positive about their service provider but negative about the service system (McWilliam 1996, Lang et al. 1995, McWilliam et al. 1995b). Affleck et al. (1989) found that a home visiting program for parents of high-risk infants increased maternal perception of having control over life events.

Bailey et al. (1998) provide a stimulating analysis of the shift needed in research to document outcomes centered on the family. They remind us that a "major policy issue yet to be determined is the relative importance of child versus family outcomes." One perplexing scenario, they point out, might be one in which the child makes little progress, but much has changed in the family.

*Education of the Handicapped Act Amendments of 1986, Public Law 99-457, 34 CFR, Part 303, Part H, Federal Register, 54(119), 26306-26348, June 22, 1989.

Examples of Research with Specific Populations

- **Pre-term infants**
Heriza and Sweeney (1990) discuss implications for practitioners of development intervention for pre-term infants in a neonatal intensive care unit (NICU) and summarize that the NICU intervention enhanced the development of pre-term infants when the caregiver and infant were active participants. They also conclude that the infants who received both NICU intervention and a home-based program had better developmental outcomes than infants in only one type of program. These authors, as well as Bennett (1995), concur that there are many weaknesses in the studies that have examined the effectiveness of intervention in the NICU. Bennett indicates that the benefits of one particular intervention protocol are often not replicated in other investigations. That makes it difficult, if not impossible, to generalize recommendations about the approach that should be used.

Als (1997) describes other first generation and second generation research completed with infants in neonatal intensive care units. Als indicates that the second generation research focuses on the family-centered model of care used in most NICUs. Some of the studies summarized by Als demonstrate success measured by reduced length of stay, improved weight gain, fewer medical complications, and improved developmental outcomes.

- **Children exposed prenatally to drugs and/or alcohol**
Olson and Burgess (1997) summarize research in this area and indicate that we have learned some factors that help make drug-exposed children more resilient. These include:

    a. nonjudgmental attitudes on the part of professionals

    b. early success in improving infants' self regulation and mutual regulation between the child and caregiver

    c. availability of a responsive and safe care environment

    d. specialized support for caregivers and professionals

    e. the use of a primary service provider rather than having large numbers of service providers

The research also indicates that there are certain ways to handle these babies to reduce irritability (e.g., swaddling, rocking beds). The researchers point out how important it is for interventionists to recognize and understand the behavioral characteristics of children with alcohol-related birth defects. This allows the provider to view the learning and behavior problems as part of the CNS dysfunction.

- **Children born to mothers with mental retardation**
Feldman et al. (1993) evaluated the effectiveness of a home-based parent-training program for mothers with mental retardation on the language

development of their children under the age of 28 months. Training the mothers how to work with their children had a significant positive impact on the children's language skills.

- **High-risk infants**
Haney and Klein (1993) reported on the Mother-Infant Communication Project, a program designed to facilitate caregivers' uses of communicative interaction strategies with infants labeled as high-risk. The mothers who received intervention were better at using communicative interaction strategies than comparison group mothers. In addition, the infants of mothers who received a group experience in addition to home visits performed significantly better on a language measure at 18 months of age.

- **Children with Down syndrome**
Spiker and Hopmann (1997) reported longitudinal studies of children with Down syndrome, indicating that the overall mental ages of the majority of older children with Down syndrome tend to be early school-age level. Some studies indicate that infants with Down syndrome make slower progress compared with children who have other disabilities or delays. Some studies indicate that adolescents with Down syndrome who receive early intervention score higher on IQ testing than age-matched adolescents who do not receive this intervention, though Spiker and Hopmann acknowledge weaknesses in the design of such studies. Because development is slower for children with Down syndrome, Spiker and Hopmann indicate that it is difficult to implement an intervention and collect outcome data.

- **Children with autism**
Dawson and Osterling (1997) describe early intervention for infants and children with autism. They describe examples of model early intervention programs for these children. They conclude that all of the programs were effective in obtaining positive school placements, reaching significant developmental gains, or both. For example, about half of the children were able to be integrated into a general classroom by the end of intervention. They also showed gains in IQ.

- **Children with hearing loss**
Yoshinaga-Itano et al. (1998) found that children identified with hearing loss by six months of age who received appropriate intervention had significantly better language skills (receptive and expressive) than children identified after six months of age. This sample controlled for cognition. The better language skills were evident regardless of other factors like gender, ethnicity, degree of hearing loss, mode of communication, or presence or absence of other disabilities. The study found no differences in language scores between four later-identified subgroups (7 months to 25 months), suggesting that the six-month age may be a critical age to identify children if optimal language development is to occur.

Studies have documented that when parents are hearing and children are deaf or hard of hearing, the interactions between children and their parents are less than optimal. Pressman (1998) found that ratings of the mother's emotional availability (which tap into sensitivity and teaching ability) had more of an impact on predicting which children would make significant language gains when the children were deaf or hard of hearing compared to children with normal hearing. She concluded that the language of children who are deaf or hard of hearing is more responsive to greater maternal sensitivity.

Another study by Yoshinaga-Itano (2000) found that newborn hearing screening programs for hearing loss were positively related to scores in expressive and receptive language, vocabulary production, and speech intelligibility.

Moeller (2000) found that children enrolled earliest (e.g., by 11 months of age) demonstrated significantly better vocabulary and verbal reasoning skills at five years of age than the children enrolled later in a comprehensive intervention program. Family involvement explained this variance, underscoring the importance of this component. In other words, children enrolled earlier had more family involvement and for a longer period of time.

Effectiveness of intervention for children with communication disorders

Stark (1995) indicates that the evidence suggests that early language intervention is effective when it is designed to meet the needs of the individual child. She advises that when making a decision about when to intervene and how best to intervene, the clinician consider:

- risk factors
- predisposing conditions
- child's pattern of deficits
- severity of the language impairment

Warren and Kaiser (1986) reviewed incidental language teaching, defined as "the interactions between an adult and a child that arise naturally in an unstructured situation . . .." They concluded that incidental teaching:

- teaches target skills in the natural environment
- results in generalization of the skills
- results in gains in formal aspects of language
- results in gains in functional aspects of language

Kaiser et al. (1991) conclude that milieu teaching (i.e., a broad, naturalistic approach) can be used successfully to teach specific language skills. Milieu teaching includes identifying appropriate language targets, arranging the environment and materials to trigger child-initiated communication, and responding to the communication or to the intent of the communication.

McLean and Cripe (1997) reviewed 56 studies of language intervention for young children (though many of these studies involved children over the age of three). They organized these studies into those in which:

- a single intervention approach was implemented by a professional in a center or clinic setting

- two or more intervention approaches were compared

- home-based intervention was provided with the parent as the primary interventionist (Note: The only studies summarized involved children over the age of 36 months and are thus not reported here.)

Highlighted findings from some of those studies that involved children under the age of three are summarized here from the first two categories above.

Single intervention approach, clinic, or center
Warren et al. (1993) found that the subjects increased their rate of target responses during milieu intervention and generalized these responses to new settings. Yoder et al. (1994) found that the subjects increased their rate of intentional requesting and generalized this to other sessions with their mothers.

Comparison studies
Wilcox et al. (1991) found significantly higher rates of generalized word production in the home setting when the children were seen in the classroom rather than in the therapy room. Mahoney and Powell (1988) found significant language improvements when the parent used specific interaction and turn-taking techniques as trained in weekly home visits. There was also a positive relationship between the parents' use of these techniques (interaction and turn-taking) and the child's overall rate of gain on the *Bayley Mental Development Index* (MDI). Whitehurst et al. (1991) also found improved scores on standardized tests for children whose parents were taught facilitation techniques.

McLean and Cripe concluded that the data available does not allow prediction of when direct intervention by a SLP will be the most effective approach compared to intervention provided by teachers or parents. They also acknowledge the increased need for information about services provided to children under the age of three. Keep in mind that many of the studies reviewed by McLean and Cripe involved children over the age of 36 months.

Ward (1999) reported on a study involving 122 very young, language-delayed children. The sample was divided into matched experimental and control groups. The experimental group received intervention similar to milieu teaching. Ward reported extremely positive results, with 85 percent of controls showing language delay at three years of age and only 5 percent of the experimental group showing language delays. However, numerous researchers (Hall 1999, Letts & Edwards 1999, Yoder 1999) have pointed out the weaknesses in the research design of Ward's study, including possible observer bias, outcome measure used, number of subjects, method of intervention studied, and practice effects of taking a test over and over again.

Summary

The evidence base for early intervention services is growing. More research concerning specific approaches and techniques needs to be completed. Clinicians working in the area of early intervention should stay abreast of current findings and adjust service delivery accordingly.

Chapter 4

Medical Disorders and Syndromes Associated with Children Birth to Three

by Sarah Shoemaker Shields

This chapter is a reference guide to provide a brief overview of a variety of medical disorders, syndromes, and problems that are encountered when evaluating and treating children in the birth-to-three age range. It is not intended to be a comprehensive review of each disorder, nor is it intended to provide information on all of the different disorders you may encounter. This chapter might be useful when you receive a new referral and want to look up a little information about the child's medical problems before you conduct your evaluation. (See Appendix 4A, page 46, for a list of resource books with more detailed information.)

Chromosomal/Genetic Disorders

Cri du Chat

Cri du Chat is a genetic disorder that occurs when a portion of the short arm on chromosome 5 is deleted. Microcephaly, congenital heart defects, and severe hypotonicity are some of the defining characteristics, as is the characteristic high-pitched cry that has been compared to the meowing of a cat. In French "cri du chat" means "cry of the cat." The associated hypotonicity affects multiple systems and leads to feeding, respiratory, and motor difficulties. In infancy, children with Cri du Chat may present as failure to thrive due to the degree of feeding difficulties. Communicative abilities will be dependent upon the degree of mental retardation and the presence of cleft lip/palate, which is not uncommon. Total lack of speech development, however, is typical.

Down syndrome

Down syndrome is a genetic disorder caused by a chromosomal abnormality in which there is an extra 21st chromosome, thus resulting in its other name, *Trisomy 21*. The characteristics of Down syndrome vary but may include:

- slanted eyes
- hypothyroidism
- congenital heart defects
- short stature
- small facial features
- epicanthal folds (small folds of skin from the upper eyelid to the corner of the eye)
- flattened back of head
- short, broad hands
- joint hyperflexibility
- hypotonia
- mental retardation

In addition, children with Down syndrome often have characteristic oral abnormalities that contribute to articulation and feeding issues, including small mouth, large tongue with a forward carriage and restricted movement, and malocclusions.

Fragile X

Fragile X is an X-linked genetic disorder. It is the second leading cause of mental retardation and primarily affects males. The mental retardation ranges from mild to severe. The associated facial features include an elongated face, drooping eyelids, and prominence of the forehead, nose, jaw, and ears. Individuals with Fragile X are at increased risk for cleft palate and thus, the associated feeding and speech difficulties that may occur as the result of a cleft.

There is also a high incidence of ADHD and autistic-type behaviors in these individuals. Sensory integration issues also frequently occur in children with Fragile X. Communication abilities are dependent upon the severity of mental retardation. A team approach to treating individuals with Fragile X is most effective, utilizing a SLP, OT, and PT to facilitate the development of communication, sensory, and motor issues.

Klinefelter Syndrome

This is a genetic disorder affecting males only, in which there is at least one extra X chromosome, but may be as many as four. The severity of its associated characteristics increases with the number of X chromosomes present. Its characteristics include a small penis and testes, female-like breasts, obesity, tall stature, poor coordination, and delayed social development. These children may have self-esteem issues as a result of these physical characteristics.

According to Gerber (1998), 75% of individuals with Klinefelter have delayed development of language and phonological skills. Language processing disorders are also common as these children have poor auditory memories.

Klinefelter is not typically diagnosed until school age. However, if there is a definitive diagnosis prior to entrance into school, the early interventionist should focus on facilitating the development of both expressive and receptive language.

Prader Willi

This disorder is characterized by small, almond-shaped eyes; strabismus; a low forehead; slow height growth; and hypotonia. In the majority of cases, Prader Willi is caused by a genetic defect occurring on chromosome 15. As infants, children with Prader Willi may present as failure to thrive, however, between the ages of one and three, obesity becomes a defining characteristic.

Children with Prader Willi are of varying intelligence. The IQ range is quite broad. Articulation disorders and feeding disorders are not uncommon in these children due to poor oral-motor strength and function secondary to hypotonia. Velopharyngeal incompetence may also be an issue as a result of hypotonia.

Because mental retardation and learning disabilities are possible with Prader Willi, receptive and expressive language may warrant intervention.

Stickler Syndrome

Stickler Syndrome is a disorder of the connective tissue, resulting in bone and joint problems. The associated characteristics include:

- underdeveloped facial features, especially the chin

- long and thin extremities

- glossoptosis (downward disposition or retraction of the tongue)

- conductive and/or sensorineural hearing loss. Chronic otitis media has implications for language learning.

Children with Stickler may have an overt or submucous cleft contributing to early feeding disorders, as well as articulation and resonance disorders later in life. Frequently, there are associated vision problems. Feeding should be a primary concern in the birth-to-three population due to the high incidence of palatal and pharyngeal abnormalities. Velopharyngeal incompetence may also be of concern, secondary to the high incidence of cleft palate.

Treacher Collins

Treacher Collins is an autosominal dominant disorder characterized by distinctive facial and oral abnormalities, including flat cheekbones, an underdeveloped mandible, open bite with underdeveloped teeth, and other malocclusions. Sometimes there is an unusual pattern of hair growth on the face and cheeks. There is a high incidence of cleft palate in individuals with Treacher Collins. Hearing loss is also common, and is frequently bilateral and conductive due to structural abnormalities of the outer and middle ear. Significant respiratory problems are also frequently associated with Treacher Collins and children may have a tracheostomy when young.

Feeding, swallowing, and articulation disorders are common in these children because of the associated oral deficits. Additionally, hearing loss contributes to language issues, though children with Treacher Collins may be of average intelligence.

Turner Syndrome

Turner Syndrome is a chromosomal disorder, also commonly known as XO Syndrome. This syndrome affects females only and is characterized by excessive skin or webbing of the neck. Other associated characteristics include micrognathia (underdeveloped chin), a narrow maxilla and palate, hearing loss, and mental retardation. There is also a high incidence of infertility. Speech problems are common in these individuals due to oral abnormalities and associated hearing loss. Expressive and receptive language deficits likely exist due to decreased cognition.

Usher Syndrome

Usher Syndrome is a genetic disorder and the leading cause of deafness and blindness. Retinitis pigmentosa (degeneration of the retinas in both eyes) leads to varying degrees of visual impairment (Coleman 1993) and severe sensorineural hearing loss leads to speech and language delays. Augmentative communication may be necessary, though it should not rely heavily on visual skills, as eventual vision loss is likely.

Velocardiofacial Syndrome (VCFS)

Velocardiofacial Syndrome is a fairly common genetic disorder with over 170 different traits. VCFS results when there is partial deletion of the 22nd chromosome. VCFS is the most common disorder with an associated submucous or overt cleft palate. Some common characteristics include heart defects, frequent otitis media, small stature, and hearing impairment. Babies with VCFS may frequently present as failure to thrive due to associated feeding difficulties.

Facial features may include a small, elongated face; small, almond-shaped eyes; micrognathia (underdeveloped chin); and a long, tubular nose. Feeding difficulties are common, particularly when there is clefting of the palate, and also due to pharyngeal hypotonicity, weak sucking pattern, and associated nasal regurgitation and gastro-esophageal reflux (Richard and Hoge 1999).

ADHD and mental retardation occur in approximately 40% of this population (Gerber 1998). Articulation disorders and hypernasality are common, due to palatal, pharyngeal, and other oral abnormalities. Language-specific deficits in the areas of auditory memory and processing are noted (Shprintzen 1997). Reading comprehension may also be affected. Early intervention should focus on feeding, cognition, and language development.

Neurological Disorders

Angelman's Syndrome

Angelman's Syndrome is a neurological disorder that is caused by partial deletion of chromosome 15 about half the time. Its characteristics include microcephaly; a prominent chin; fair, deep-set eyes; light-colored hair; and a large, wide-open mouth with irregularly spaced teeth. Because of its unusual facial characteristics, this is sometimes called the "happy puppet syndrome."

Children with Angelman's Syndrome are largely nonverbal. For those children who are able to speak, their vocabularies consist of very few words. These children typically suffer severe cognitive impairment, have feeding issues and poor oral skills secondary to structural anomalies, and may experience an associated seizure disorder.

Cerebral Palsy (CP)

Cerebral Palsy is a non-progressive disorder of muscle control or coordination that may occur as the result of both genetic and/or acquired factors. CP may occur as the result of brain damage sustained during fetal life, the newborn period, or early childhood. Causes of brain damage may include prenatal drug/alcohol abuse, maternal infection during pregnancy, an inadequate supply of oxygen during labor or delivery, brain infections including meningitis or encephalitis, or head injury. The symptoms and type of CP that result are dependent upon the location of the brain damage.

The three types of cerebral palsy are pyramidal, extrapyramidal, and mixed. The common traits are impaired muscle tone and incoordination, spasticity, dyskinesia (unwanted, involuntary motor movements), and ataxia. Motor milestones are obviously delayed in children with CP, and 60-70% of individuals have mental retardation, depending on the location and severity of brain damage (Healy 1984). Cerebral palsy is the leading cause of dysphagia in children.

Landau Kleffner

Landau Kleffner, sometimes referred to as "acquired epileptic aphasia," is a rare disorder characterized by a rapid decline in previously acquired speech and language skills. Children may be normally developing until three to seven years of age, then experience a notable decline in their abilities to communicate. Landau Kleffner may first be detected by an abnormal EEG due to associated seizures, and with the emergence of autistic-like behaviors. Because Landau Kleffner does not typically occur before the age of three, it may not be a disorder encountered by the early interventionist, however, it is a disorder worthy of mention in the event that these symptoms begin to appear during the toddler years.

Congenital Malformations

Cleft lip and/or palate

The roof and front of the mouth are formed during the 6th through 13th week of gestation as soft tissues develop and bony processes fuse at midline. A disruption of this process may result in cleft lip and/or palate. Severity of the cleft is dependent upon the timing of the interruption during fetal development. Clefting may be of the lip and palate or may occur singly. Clefting may be unilateral or bilateral.

Cleft palate alone (i.e., without accompanying cleft lip) is often part of a syndrome (e.g., Pierre Robin). Hardy (1984) lists complications that may result from cleft lip and/or palate:

- dental problems/malocclusions
- susceptibility to upper respiratory infections
- middle ear disease (otitis media) and associated hearing impairment due to improperly functioning Eustachian tubes
- feeding difficulties and nutritional problems during infancy/early years
- speech deficits
- psychological problems due to low self-esteem
- educational issues due to health, hearing, and psychological problems

Children with cleft lip/palate should first be referred to a cleft palate team, center, or specialist to make initial decisions regarding medical management and surgical repair. The SLP should work closely with other team members regarding feeding issues, including feeding techniques and the need for special feeding equipment. The SLP should closely monitor speech development, and be aware of possible velopharygeal insufficiency and make referrals for VPI testing as indicated.

Pierre Robin

Pierre Robin is a congenital disorder characterized by an underdeveloped lower jaw, cleft palate, and feeding difficulties due to displacement of the tongue. There is a high incidence of airway obstruction that may contribute to pharyngeal dysphagia, aspiration, and/or death. The young child may have to undergo tracheostomy. Cleft palate contributes to feeding difficulties. Structural abnormalities may also lead to articulation disorders and velopharyngeal insufficiency.

Atypical Development

Pervasive Developmental Disorders (PDD)/Autism Spectrum

Although disorders falling under the PDD category may go undiagnosed until later in childhood, it is important to be aware of the types and defining characteristics that may emerge during the toddler years so that the early interventionist can provide parents with appropriate education and make recommendations/referrals as warranted.

Asperger's Syndrome

The term *Asperger's Syndrome* falls under the category of Pervasive Developmental Disorders. It is often used synonymously with high-functioning autism. However, according to Trevarthen et al. (1996), Asperger's characteristics are more consistent with right hemisphere deficits while high-functioning autism characteristics are more consistent with left-hemisphere language communication deficits. Children with Asperger's are typically of normal intelligence and present with the following behavioral characteristics as described by Wing (in Attwood 1998):

- lack of empathy
- naiveté
- inappropriate, one-sided interaction
- little or no ability to form friendships
- echolalic, repetitive speech
- poor nonverbal communication
- intense absorption in certain subjects
- clumsy, poorly-coordinated movements

Children with Asperger's have significant difficulties with social interaction and therefore, may seek the company of younger children or adults who are more accepting and tolerant of their unusual behaviors. Their speech may be monotone and devoid of facial expression. Figurative language may be a challenge because these children are literal thinkers. They may have difficulty with humor and sarcasm because it is too abstract.

Autism

Autism is a developmental, neurological disorder. Children with autism have poor social interaction, difficulty establishing relationships, and may avoid interacting with others. They are resistant to change and engage in self-stimulation behaviors, including hand flapping and rocking. According to Richard & Hoge (1999), it is not unusual for children with autism to present with higher expressive language skills than receptive language skills due to the nature of their learning. These children learn songs, memorize commercials, and deliver lines from their favorite movies, often repeating them over and over throughout the course of a day and to everyone they encounter. Expressively though, there is very little meaningful output. Pragmatic skills are poor because children with autism are unable to communicate in various contexts, often do not use eye contact or facial expressions, and do not understand social rules.

Failure to Thrive (FTT)

A condition of infancy and early childhood characterized by lower weight/slower weight gain than that expected by comparison to a standardized growth chart (Coleman 1993). Children may present as failure to thrive due to malnourishment as a result of negative psychological/environmental (non-organic) or physical conditions (organic). Physical causes of FTT may include various syndromes/disorders, cardiovascular, and/or digestive issues. Non-organic or environmental causes may include poverty, ignorance, poor parent-child interactions, abuse, and/or neglect. Children who are malnourished will have poor learning capacity, limited attention, and decreased short-term memory. As a result, language learning may be an issue. The early interventionist may need to consult with a dietician in addition to focusing on feeding techniques to facilitate proper nourishment.

Environmental Disorders and Other Medical Factors

Fetal Alcohol Syndrome (FAS)

Fetal Alcohol Syndrome is an accumulation of congenital abnormalities resulting from maternal alcohol use/abuse during pregnancy. The result of FAS may be slow physical growth, mental retardation, delayed fine and gross motor development, and attention issues (ADD/ADHD). Children with FAS may have characteristic facial traits, including small eyes, nose, and jaw; epicanthal folds; and thin upper lip. FAS is one of the leading causes of mental retardation (Schultz 1984) and therefore may cause language delays, learning issues, and overall developmental delay.

Otitis Media

Otitis media results when there is inflammation of the middle ear, which may be caused by an upper respiratory infection. Chronic inflammation causes fluid to collect in the eustachian tubes and prevents drainage of the fluid, resulting in infection. If the condition is chronic, it may impact hearing and thus impact speech and language development.

Otitis media is common among children under six years of age and frequently occurs in ages birth to three, the time frame that is critical to speech and language development. The early interventionist must educate parents regarding the importance of hearing assessment in children with chronic ear infections, as well as the importance of regular visits to the physician regarding possible need for ventilation tubes and other medical management.

Prenatal Drug Exposure

Prenatal drug exposure may lead to a variety of physical, developmental, and behavioral disabilities, including prematurity, low birthweight, respiratory difficulties, tachycardia, hypertonia, seizure disorders, feeding issues, and abnormal sleep patterns (Rossetti 2001). The degree and severity of these problems is dependent upon the type of substance and dosage used during pregnancy. Marijuana and cocaine are the most frequent substances abused by expectant mothers, placing infants at extreme risk for medical issues and therefore, developmental risk.

Not only are physical and developmental factors need for concern, but also the environment and parenting styles in the home setting. The early interventionist should familiarize herself with the specifics of the child's prenatal and perinatal history and be aware that prenatal drug exposure will likely contribute to developmental delay, specifically in the areas of cognition and communication. Rivers and Hendrick (1992) list communication issues:

- limited expressive language
- increased use of gesture
- reduced word retrieval ability
- disorganized sentence construction
- lack of turn taking
- reduced pragmatic skills
- limited overall vocabulary
- reduced attention span
- increased distractibility

Tracheostomy

Children with neuromuscular and/or congenital disorders, craniofacial anomalies, tracheoesophageal abnormalities, and other medical complications may require placement of a tracheostomy. A tracheostomy tube is inserted through an incision into the trachea to create an open airway. Placement of the tracheostomy allows for pulmonary suctioning, mechanical ventilation, and avoidance of upper airway obstruction.

Speech and language therapy for the young child should focus on the development of an early communication system as well as establishing vocalizations. Occlusion of the cannula is an efficient means of establishing early vocalizations. Another option to achieve voicing is the Passy-Muir Tracheostomy Speaking Valve. Neither of these methods should be used until the SLP has consulted with the child's physician to assure that this occlusion will not impair the child's respiratory function. Augmentative/alternative communication options during the early years may include sign language, picture boards, and artificial speech via an electrolarynx.

Additionally, children with tracheostomies are at risk for dysphagia. Presence of the tracheostomy may hinder laryngeal movement and therefore, put the child at risk for aspiration. An instrumental evaluation of swallowing may be indicated to assess pharyngeal swallowing function. A specialized feeding program, including modified food consistencies and individualized feeding techniques, may be necessary.

Sensory Disorders

Hearing Impairment

Hearing impairment can range in severity from mild to profound and is classified as either conductive or sensorineural. When both types are present, the loss type is mixed.

> *Conductive hearing loss* is the result of a dysfunction in the outer or middle ear.
>
> *Sensorineural loss* is the result of damage to the inner ear or auditory nerve.

Hearing loss may be unilateral or bilateral. The most common cause of conductive loss is otitis media. (See Otitis Media in the Environmental Disorders section, page 43.) Sensorineural loss may be congenital or a result of maternal infection during pregnancy or acquired during delivery as the result of traumatic birth, including anoxia or head injury. Acquired sensorineural loss may occur with certain infectious diseases or may result from head trauma or exposure to extraordinarily loud noises.

Early identification and appropriate intervention can minimize the impact of hearing loss on a child's development. Children suspected of hearing loss should be taken for a full audiological evaluation as soon as possible. Conductive loss caused by ear infections can be medically managed, generally with regular appointments with the physician for bouts of otitis media. Children with severe hearing impairment will miss out on early auditory experiences and will likely exhibit language delay. The child with hearing impairment should be enrolled in early intervention programs specifically designed for children with hearing impairments.

Visual Impairment

Visual acuity develops gradually with age. For normal vision to occur, images must be accurately transmitted to the brain. A simplified description of the visual process includes light passing into the cornea through the iris, which opens and closes to regulate light. The light passes through the lens to the retina, which changes it into signals that can be transmitted via the optic nerve and processed by the brain. Visual impairment results when any one of these steps is interrupted.

For the young child with visual impairment, it is crucial to ensure that she attains the skills to develop a solid foundation for communication and learning. According to Zambone (1995), there are several aspects of language that should be addressed, including:

- vocabulary development
- expressions of feelings
- self-image and conceptual statements
- sound localization and discrimination
- sound-symbol associations

In the cognitive domain, intervention should address concept development including spatial relationships, causality, object permanence, generalization, and symbolic representation. Early intervention is key to minimize the developmental delay that may occur in a child with visual impairment.

Infectious Diseases

Fetal Cytomegalovirus Syndrome (CMV)

Cytomegalovirus is a disorder in the herpes virus group. Associated characteristics may include microcephaly, mental retardation, obstructive hydrocephalus, optic atrophy, chorioretinitis (inflammation of the retina), and hearing impairment. Otoneurological complications resulting from CMV may include invasion of the cochlea and semicircular canals as well as structures of the central auditory nervous system, including the cochlear nuclei and cerebral cortex (Jung 1989). This invariably results in sensorineural hearing impairment. The hearing impairment may range from mild to profound and may be either bilateral or unilateral.

CMV, depending on the severity of associated hearing loss and mental retardation, may impact speech and language development. Early intervention for children with CMV will maximize the development of speech and language skills.

Summary

It is important for professionals providing early intervention services to be aware of the many types of medical disorders that may be seen in infants and young children. This information will help the interventionist understand prognosis and establish treatment goals accordingly. In addition, it allows the professional to discuss the child's associated problems with the caregivers.

Appendix 4A

Resources

Medical Aspects of Developmental Disabilities in Children Birth to Three
J. Blackman, 1984
Pro-Ed

Treatment Options in Early Intervention
J. Blackman, 1995
Aspen Publishers

The Early Intervention Dictionary: A Multidisciplinary Guide to Terminology
J. Coleman, 1993
Woodbine House

The Source for Syndromes
G. Richard & D. Hoge, 1999
LinguiSystems, Inc.

The Source for Syndromes 2
G. Richard & D. Hoge, 2000
LinguiSystems, Inc.

Communication Intervention Birth to Three, Second Edition
L. Rossetti, 2001
Delmar Publishing

Chapter 5

Tools and Methods for Assessment

Assessment of the child provides the foundation for treatment planning. Assessment takes place before intervention is initiated but is also an ongoing process throughout the course of intervention.

What Is Assessment?

Rossetti (1990b) defines assessment as "any activity, either formal (through the use of norm-referenced, standardized criteria) or informal (through the use of developmental profiles or checklists) that is designed to elicit accurate and reliable samples of infant-toddler behavior upon which inferences relative to developmental skill status may be made." He also points out that what determines an effective assessor of communication skills is "not the ability to administer tests, but rather the clinical skills necessary to interpret information gained (regardless of the source of the information) and use that information in structuring an effective program of remediation" (Rossetti 2001).

Rossetti also stresses how important it is that communication assessment begins as soon in the child's life as possible. Because we know the risk factors that may result in the child presenting with a communication delay, there is no need to wait until the child is actually behind in communication development to begin assessment. The precursors to communication (e.g., interaction, attachment, play, pragmatics, gesture) can form the basis for early assessment.

Assessing a young child

The assessment of communication and swallowing skills in children in the birth-to-three age range differs in several ways from the assessment of an older child. Often children in this age range are being evaluated because they are at risk for a communication disorder rather than because they are already presenting with a communication disorder. (The referral for assessment of feeding and swallowing is usually for a more clear-cut presenting problem.) Children below the age of three will often not participate fully in the assessment, especially if this is the first time they have met the examiner. Establishing rapport with the child is crucial to obtaining an accurate assessment.

Most assessments of children this age rely heavily on observation and caregiver report. Even when the child WILL participate, the testing must be more like play than work. It is often necessary to see the child several times before an adequate representation of his skills can be obtained. Multiple domains must be assessed, and evaluation is often multidisciplinary or transdisciplinary in nature.

The role of the SLP is to:

- Determine if there is a communication disorder.

- Describe the nature and type of the communication disorder.

- Establish baseline functioning in all areas of communication.

- Determine if the child is at high-risk to develop a communication disorder.

- Determine if there is a feeding/swallowing disorder and describe it.

- Determine if referrals are needed to other professionals concerning the communication and/or feeding/swallowing disorder.

- Use assessment data to plan appropriate intervention.

- Periodically reassess and adjust the plan of care.

Principles of Assessment

Prizant and Wetherby (1995) summarize principles of assessment important in early intervention.

Gather information about the child's communication in different situations and at different times.

Children may demonstrate a skill that is well-established in both familiar and unfamiliar situations, but an emerging skill may only be demonstrated in a well-known routine with familiar individuals. The child may exhibit different skills at home than he does at the daycare or in the clinic.

Use a number of different strategies to collect the information.

As mentioned, a child under the age of three may not be receptive to doing what the examiner wants when the examiner wants him to do it. It may be necessary to observe the child in his natural environment and interview others who know the child well to piece together an accurate picture of the child's skills. If you don't have unlimited time for observations in the natural environment, you can try to structure the environment somewhat to elicit the desired behavior. For example, if you are interested in knowing if the child answers *yes/no* questions, ask the daycare teacher to involve the child in a situation during which the teacher will ask *yes/no* questions. Using a variety of strategies will provide a better description of the child's skills.

Use a number of tools or methods for assessment.

Commercially-available tools are reviewed in Appendix 5A (pages 61–64). Many rely on different methods of testing (e.g., direct observation, parent report, elicited behaviors). Observational and developmental checklists will add important information to that obtained on a standardized or criterion-referenced tool. You can also use videotape taken in the child's natural environment for later analysis of the child's skills.

With the birth-to-three population, the caregiver interview is one of the most important tools. Since the goal is to provide services using a naturalistic model (and in a natural environment), the interview will provide crucial information for selecting goals that can be accomplished in activities of day-to-day living. In addition, the interview helps identify the needs and strengths of the family. Some suggested topics for initial interviews might include some of those described by Meisels and Provence (1989):

- Ask the caregivers what they see as the purpose of the assessment process.

- Summarize the information you have available about the child and ask the caregivers what their views are of this information.

- Ask the caregivers what their concerns are about the child.

- Ask for pertinent family information and health history.

- Ask about feeding and oral behavior.

- Ask how the child acts when he is uncomfortable, frustrated, or otherwise distressed.

- Ask about language and communication behaviors and how the child gets what he needs in the environment.

- Ask about the toys and materials the child likes best.

- Ask if there's any other information the caregivers want to share with you.

Tell the family the reason for each question you ask, as they may not understand why certain personal questions are being asked. Tell them they do not need to answer any questions that might make them uncomfortable (Noonan & McCormick 1993).

In addition to caregiver interviews, you might also use a developmental log. Ask caregivers to note each time they observe the child doing something that appears to be a new behavior (Rossetti 2001).

Select the tools based on the child's developmental level.

Don't resort to always using the same testing instrument or same methods just because the child is in the birth-to-three age range. For example, a very verbal, but unintelligible 2½-year-old, may need a phonological assessment. A compliant child may show most of his skills in a structured testing situation while a more recalcitrant child may need to be assessed almost totally through observation or parent report.

Assess conventional and unconventional communicative behavior.

Children with significant delays in the development of conventional communication (speech and gestures) may be communicating in less conventional ways (e.g., biting a playmate who has taken a toy, throwing a tantrum when made to come to the table). These are forms of communication and should be noted.

Rely on caregivers as being the experts on the child's communicative abilities.

The caregivers know the child best and can provide valuable information about the child's skills. They are with the child the most, and have observed the child's communication skills in a variety of situations. Trust their descriptions of the child's behaviors as they may have observed emergent skills you have not seen.

Use developmental research to provide a framework for assessment.

A clear understanding of normal development of communication and swallowing skills will help you place the child's level of functioning on a developmental continuum.

Tie assessment results to intervention planning.

It is apparent that the results of the evaluation should form the basis for the intervention plan that is developed. In addition, ongoing evaluation is crucial because children develop new skills rapidly in the infant-toddler years.

Home-based vs. Center-based Assessments

As discussed in Chapters 1 and 2, services are being provided more frequently in the natural environment, often the home. Completing an assessment in the home provides several advantages as summarized by Filler (1983):

- The parents feel comfortable and may act more naturally.

- Children may perform better in the familiar environment.

- Behaviors can be elicited in an environment in which they typically occur.

- If the child is medically fragile, his health is better protected.

- The family's routines are less interrupted, allowing you to obtain a more accurate picture of child-caregiver interaction.

- More family members may be present who can give information about the child.

Filler contrasted these results with some advantages to center-based assessment services:

- Additional professional expertise is readily available and the child might be evaluated by a team.

- Parents have the opportunity to interact with other parents.

- Any specialized services needed are more readily available in a center.

Models of Assessment

Particularly in a center-based program, team models of assessment may be used. Different models include:

- **Multidisciplinary Approach**
  Each professional may assess the child individually. Separate reports are usually generated and intervention tends to be discipline specific.

- **Interdisciplinary Approach**
  This is a more cooperative approach. Discipline-specific assessments are completed, but then the professionals meet as a team to discuss their findings and plan treatment based on team consensus.

- **Transdisciplinary Approach**
  This team model involves a conscious effort to share information about the child. The child is usually assessed in an arena format simultaneously by many professionals. For example, the physical therapist engages the child in activities while the SLP, OT, and developmental interventionist observe. The physical therapist elicits behaviors in areas that may be outside her scope of practice, such as specific communicative behaviors, fine motor behaviors, and cognitive behaviors. The other professionals record the child's responses.

- **Transdisciplinary Play-Based Assessment**
  Linder (1990) describes the approach in this way: "Transdisciplinary play-based assessment (TPBA) involves the child in structured and unstructured play situations with, at varying times, a facilitating adult, the parent(s), and another child or children. Designed for children functioning between the ages of six months to six years of age, TPBA provides an opportunity for developmental observations of social-emotional, cognitive, language and communication, and sensorimotor domains." Such an approach points out the importance of having parents actively involved throughout the process. The play-based assessment can also be less threatening to the family and less stressful for the child.

Cultural and Linguistic Sensitivity

Regardless of the testing instrument selected or model of assessment used, the collection and interpretation of the information must be sensitive to the linguistic and cultural norms of the child and his family.

Areas to Assess

Interaction, Attachment, Play, and Pragmatics

It is especially important to not only assess the relationship between the infant and caregiver (interaction and attachment), but to assess play skills and early pragmatic skills with the pre-linguistic child, as these are indicators of early communication development. Ogletree and Daniels (1995) highlight the importance of assessing pre-linguistic communication development, particularly social communication that develops in the pre-language period of birth to 18 months of age. The three stages of early communicative growth are summarized on the next page.

- Perlocutionary (birth–8 months)
Children's actions are pre-intentional but may have systematic effects on the listener. That is, the caregiver may interpret a cry as indicating hunger or pain.

- Illocutionary (9–12 months)
Children gesture and vocalize purposefully to express their needs and desires.

- Locutionary (13–18 months)
Children demonstrate intentional use of symbols, typically referential words. These communicative intentions may be for the purposes of behavioral regulation, social interaction, or joint attention.

The table below lists assessment targets for pre-linguistic children. It is good to keep these more general targets in mind as you administer other kinds of tests that focus on evaluating discrete skills. For example, you won't find an item "Caregiver is sensitive to child's behaviors" on most instruments, but it is an important aspect of the evaluation.

Assessment Targets for Pre-linguistic Children

Perlocutionary Functioning
• Physical Competence
    hearing
    vision
    vocal development
    gestural development (upper extremity movement)
 	
• Behaviors
    affective displays (positive and negative)
    gaze shifts
    attempts to gain and share attention
    turn taking within social exchanges
 	
• Caregiver Variables
    sensitivity to child behaviors
    consistency of responses to child behaviors
    provision of communicative functioning

Illocutionary and Locutionary Functioning
• Expression of Communicative Intent
    communicative intentions
    communicative means (e.g., gestures, vocalizations)
 	
• Symbolic Abilities
    comprehension of words and simple word combinations
    use of words and simple word combinations
    number of words
    types of words and word combinations
    phonetic composition of words
    single and multiple play action schemes

Reprinted with permission. Ogletree, B. T. & Daniels, D. B. (1995). Communication-based assessment and intervention for pre-linguistic infants and toddlers: Strategies and issues. In J. A. Blackman (Ed.), *Identification and assessment in early intervention, 5, 3,* 225-229.

Ogletree and Daniels also list indicators of possible communication impairment in pre-linguistic children.

Indicators of Possible Communication Impairment in Pre-linguistic Children
Perlocutionary Functioning • Demographic Factors 　　sex (typically males) 　　later birth order 　　family history • Perinatal History 　　very low birthweight (less than 1.5kg) • Interactional Variables 　　poor visual discrimination 　　limited turn taking
Illocutionary and Locutionary Functioning • Communicative Behaviors 　　low or high rates of communication 　　predominant use of regulatory communicative intentions 　　predominant use of gestures 　　limited use of isolated vocalizations 　　limited use of respondent communicative acts 　　few comments 　　increased maladaptive behaviors 　　reduced phonologic maturity

Reprinted with permission. Ogletree, B. T. & Daniels, D. B. (1995). Communication-based assessment and intervention for pre-linguistic infants and toddlers: Strategies and issues. In J. A. Blackman (Ed.), *Identification and assessment in early intervention, 5,* 3, 225-229.

Play skills are thought to reflect early cognitive development, and thus are important to assess. There are two basic ways to assess play:

- Free-play observation
  Observe the child playing at home or in another natural setting. Depending on the age of the child, it may be important to observe him playing with peers.

- Structured elicitation (Bond et al. 1990)
  Present the child with certain toys and maybe ask him to perform certain actions.

Westby (1980) showed the relationship between the development of play behaviors and communication skills that develop at the same age. Parts of that scale are reprinted in the Appendix 5B (page 65).

Pragmatics is the use of language in social contexts. Pragmatics as assessed in the young child are closely linked to interaction behaviors and can be viewed as early expressive language in the pre-linguistic child. In the pre-linguistic child, assessment of pragmatics looks at the intention of the child's behavior as well as the child's understanding of turn taking in these early (and probably nonverbal) conversations. Some pragmatic behaviors to assess include those described by Roberts and Crais (1989):

- attention seeking
- request object
- request action
- request information
- protest
- comment on object
- comment on action
- greeting
- answering
- acknowledgement of other's speech

These authors point out the behavior the child uses to achieve the same pragmatic function changes as the child's language skills improve. For example, in the prelinguistic stage, the child may point to an object he wants. In the single-word stage, the child may name the object. In the multi-word stage, the child may use a phrase to request the object.

Language Comprehension

Comprehension is rarely assessed in isolation and is usually part of a more comprehensive assessment of all areas of language function. Many of the behaviors described above as play, interaction, and pragmatics yield information about the child's early language comprehension skills. Many of the tests described at the end of this chapter include a component for assessing language comprehension. If a less formal approach is used, it is helpful to use the guidelines provided by Chapman (1981) in the chart below.

Age	Comprehension Ability
8–12 months	understands a few single words in a routine context
12–18 months	understands single words, but outside of routine some contextual cues are needed
18–24 months	understands words for object not present and may understand some two-word combinations
24–36 months	understands three-word sentences, but needs context of past experience to determine meaning

Language Expression

As noted previously, language expression is typically assessed as part of a larger language battery. It must involve more than counting the number of words the child uses or even the average number of words in an utterance (MLU). You must assess both the means (behaviors by which the information is communicated) and the functions (the purposes for which the child communicates). Assessing the means would include vocabulary, semantics, and syntax. It is also important to assess the communication that occurs between the child and his communication partners (e.g., parents, caregivers). This aspect of assessment involves analyzing the child's turn-taking skills and the child's initiation of conversation routines (Rossetti 2001).

Sound Production/Phonology

There is a predicted course of development of sound production. If the child's developing speech is as intelligible as expected for developmental age, you might need only to ensure that development of sound production is proceeding as expected. The chart below reflects the age at which 75% or more children correctly produce the sound in the indicated position on the *Photo Articulation Test* (PAT, Pendergast et al. 1969).

Development of Correct Sound Production				
24 months	t- n- -n k- g- p- -p b-	m- -m h- ɑʊ u æ ɔ ə ɑɪ	ɛ ɑ i e ʌ ʊ o ɪ ɔɪ	
28 months	-s d- -d	-k f- -f	-ŋ j-	
32 months	-t -r	-b w-	ɝ	
36 months	s- -l	-g	ɚ	
40 months	-ʃ l-	bl- r- br-	tr- -v	
44 months	ʃ- tʃ-	-tʃ fl-		
48 months	sp- st-	kl- ð-	-ð -ʒ	
48+ months	z- -z	θ- -θ	v- ju	-dʒ dʒ-

Material from the SICD-R, Copyright © 1975, 1984 by Don Lea Hedrick, Elizabeth M. Prather and Annette R. Tobin, Copyright © 2002 by Western Psychological Services. Reprinted with permission of the publisher, Western Psychological Services, 12031 Wilshire Boulevard, Los Angeles, California, 90025, U.S.A. Not to be reprinted in whole or in part for any additional purpose without the expressed, written permission of the publisher. All rights reserved.

Before the age of three, a child may not be using enough expressive language to determine if his phonological development is proceeding as expected. On the other hand, some children may be talking enough but may be highly unintelligible. For children for whom intelligibility of speech is an issue, assessment of phonological development is important. If that is the case, then assessment utilizing a phonological test would be indicated.

Stoel-Gammon (1994) stresses that toddlers probably fall into three main categories in terms of the development of their phonology:

1. Developing as expected.

2. Development is slow, but child shows no major deviations from the patterns of normal acquisition. This child might be called "the late talker."

3. Developmental patterns deviate substantially from the norms in terms of the order of acquisition or achievement of certain milestones.

She also offers a list of red flags that she describes as cause for concern if they are persistent and widespread:

- numerous vowel errors
    24 months—some vowel errors are acceptable
    36 months—most vowels except /r/ vowels correct

- widespread deletion of initial consonants
    24 months—child should produce CV with three to four different consonants
    36 months—larger repertoire of initial consonants

- substitution of glottal consonants or /h/ for a variety of target consonants

- substitution of back consonants for front ones (especially velars for alveolars) when assimilation is not the cause

- deletion of final consonants
    24 months—lack of final consonants in a child with limited verbal productions would be expected
    36 months—all children should be producing some CVC syllables

Types of Tests

Norm-referenced and criterion-referenced tests may be used with this population. Some early intervention agencies may require that a norm-referenced test be used. A norm-referenced test allows you to interpret an individual's performance compared with a group. For the most part, direct elicitation of the desired behavior by the examiner is used in this type of test.

Criterion-referenced tests are those in which the content is determined by some specific performance dimension. Performance of an individual is assessed relative to these well-defined expectations and results indicate mastery or non-mastery in a particular domain. Rossetti (2001) provides an excellent comparison of the advantages and disadvantages of norm-referenced vs. criterion-referenced tests related to assessing this population and states that, "For children under three years, the use of norm-referenced tests (NRTs) has several significant limitations."

Advantages of Criterion-referenced Tests	Disadvantages of Norm-referenced Tests
The examiner is allowed to elicit desired behaviors in whatever manner best fits the child.	All test items have to be administered in narrowly prescribed fashion.
A sample of behaviors can be obtained and different responses by the child can be analyzed.	The way the child responds to the test items must be interpreted in a narrow way.
They provide a developmental profile or checklist of mastered skills, making it easy to plan where treatment should start.	It can be difficult to plan intervention based on norm-referenced test results.
Change is more easily reflected.	Results do not easily show change.
	For normally-developing children, correlation between norm-referenced, developmental test scores and later performance is not significant until three years of age.
	There has been little validity testing of the items on the test. (Is it measuring what it purports to measure?)
	Items are not weighted.

Wetherby and Prizant (1992) reviewed instruments and tests for the young child and pointed out the following limitations:

- The tests focus on communication milestones and forms (e.g., gestures and words) and don't pay attention to the functions of communication.

- Some rely only on observation or caregiver report.

- The tests ignore nonverbal signals (e.g., gaze, affect).

- Most provide a developmental age or quotient rather than a profile of strengths and weaknesses across domains.

Wetherby and Prizant's *Communication and Symbolic Behavior Scales* (*CSBS*) (2003) uses a different approach that addresses some of these concerns. It measures both developmental and quality aspects of preverbal and early linguistic abilities.

Adjusting for Prematurity

Many children referred for early intervention have been born prematurely, and will exhibit at least a mild delay in communication development. When assessing premature infants, it is important to adjust for this prematurity so that the child is being compared to children of similar developmental age. Rossetti (2001) recommends subtracting the degree of prematurity from chronological age expectations for children until approximately 12-15 months of age. This will result in a more accurate prediction of later developmental expectations. (See box.) This is based on a study by Siegel (1983) who found no significant differences between the predictive ability of the corrected and uncorrected scores after one year of age. However, the study was completed before the current increase in survival for very premature infants. Therefore, Rossetti recommends that for children born at 23-26 weeks gestation, adjustment continue until the child is 18-20 months of age.

> **Calculating Adjusted Age**
>
> A child born on 07-01-02 at 32 weeks gestation is 8 weeks premature. If you assess the child on 09-01-03, the child's chronological age is 14 months. The adjusted age is 12 months. The age is adjusted from a 40-week gestation period, which for this child would have been 09-01-02, if he wasn't born prematurely. Comparing that date (09-01-02) to the assessment date (09-01-03) yields an adjusted age of 12 months.

Hearing Acuity

It is essential to determine if reduced hearing (either fluctuating loss related to otitis media or sensori-neural loss) is one of the factors contributing to delay in the child's development of communication skills. In general, SLPs may not screen a child's hearing until the age of three. For the birth-to-three population, however, the SLP should ask if the child's hearing was screened as part of the newborn infant hearing screening program and find out the results. The SLP should also obtain information about any signs of reduced hearing acuity and make appropriate referrals for further evaluation.

Reassessing/Measuring Progress

After the initial assessment has guided the development of the treatment plan, it is important to continuously measure the child's progress on achieving the goals and treatment objectives listed on the plan. Serial assessment involves conducting regular assessments over regular periods of time (Rossetti 2001). A good clinician uses serial assessment during every session with a child. Such ongoing assessment is important for several reasons:

- Children are always changing, and the behaviors they exhibit on initial testing may change very quickly.

- It allows you to measure rate of change and development.

- It allows you to make ongoing decisions about the direction of the intervention.

Rossetti (2001) describes these patterns of change that may be observed in the child:

- Normal-abnormal development
  Skills are learned in a normal sequence but later than expected.

- Abnormal-abnormal development
  A widening distance is seen between where the child is functioning and where he should be functioning.

- Catch-up growth
  Accelerated rate of developmental skill mastery, reducing the gap between where the child is functioning and where he should be functioning.

- Varying developmental change
  Fluctuations in the distance between where the child is functioning and where he should be functioning. The fluctuations may be in either direction.

Noonan and McCormick (1993) describe common types of observational measurement systems that can be used for assessing behavior.

- event (frequency)—involves counting each time a behavior occurs

- duration—the length of time a behavior occurs

- interval—indicates if a behavior occurs or does not occur during a period of time

- time sampling—indicates if a behavior occurs at the moment following a specified time interval

- latency—measures the time between a prompt and the response

- rate—measures how quickly or slowly responses occur (usually measured as the number of responses per minute, per day, per week)

It is important to choose a measurement system that will accurately reflect whether the child is really performing the target skill at the criterion that has been stated in the treatment objective.

Collecting Data

How do you know when and how often to collect data to document progress? Sometimes the wording of the treatment objective specifies when data should be collected. For example, if the treatment objective states that the child will consistently use the gesture for *more* when requesting another bite of food, then the measurement should take place during meals. Since it is important to determine that the child is generalizing the use of the skill, you may also want to have measurements of the behavior taken in other eating situations, such as at a restaurant or a relative's house.

Chapter 5: Tools and Methods for Assessment

It is important to remember that when working with a young child, it isn't always practical to collect data when you had planned. For example, you may have planned to take data on the child's use of three-word phrases during a turn-taking game only to find that during this treatment session, the child is not interested in taking turns and instead only wants to read a book to you. If this is the case, you can ask the parents/caregiver to collect data to document the child's use of a particular skill. Use this technique only when necessary because it is difficult for a parent to collect data and interact with her child at the same time. You can also use parent report to collect information about how often a child is using a particular skill.

You should not try to collect data during every session on the performance of every skill. If you're adhering to the other principles for working with young children (e.g., following the child's lead), it is impractical to try to collect data after every response or utterance. It is important to stay engaged in the activity with the child.

Bricker and Cripe (1992) describe an overall measurement framework that reminds us of the different purposes of measuring progress. They describe Level One progress as measuring the child's weekly progress toward specific targets. Level Two progress, which they describe as quarterly, is probably best viewed as semi-annually since Individualized Family Service Plans (IFSPs) are written for six-month periods of time. The measurement that takes place then is to determine the child's progress toward the goals and objectives listed on the IFSP. Many early intervention programs have also moved to an annual evaluation of the child's progress (i.e., Level Three). The purpose of evaluation at this level is to determine the overall impact of the early intervention program.

Examples of Tests for Birth-to-Three Population — Appendix 5A

Test Name	Area(s) Assessed	Norm- or Criterion-referenced	Age Range	Notes	Author/Publisher
AEPS Test for Birth to Three Years	Fine motor, gross motor, cognitive, adaptive, social-communication, social	C	Birth to 3-0 years	Curriculum-based; assess one child or a group of children in home or at a center	Bricker 1993 Paul H. Brookes Publishing Co.
Arizona Articulation Proficiency Scale	Articulation	C/N	Any age (norms for 3-0 to 11-11 years)	Picture identification	Fudala 1970 Western Psychological Services
Assessing Pre-linguistic and Early Linguistic Behaviors in Developmentally Young Children	Cognitive, play, communicative intent, comprehension, and production	C	9 to 24 months	Observation and elicited	Olswang, Stoel-Gammon, Coggins, & Carpenter 1987 University of Washington Press
Battelle Developmental Inventory (BDI)	Personal-social, adaptive, motor, communication, cognitive	N	Birth to 8-0 years	Screening component and full battery; structured test format, interviews, and observations	Newborg, Stock, Wnek, Guidabaldi, & Svinicki 1984, 2004 Riverside Publishing
Bayley Scales of Infant Development	Mental Scale and Motor Scale	N	2 to 30 months	Item administration and observation	Bayley 1969 Psychological Corporation
Birth to Three Developmental Scales	Problem solving, personal-social skills, motor skills, general receptive and expressive language	N	Birth to 3-0 years	Observation, following directions, motor and verbal imitation, picture identification, naming body parts, object identification, parent report	Bangs & Dodson 1979 Teaching Resources
Bromwich Play Assessment Checklist for Infants	Cognitive functions, social/linguistic behavior	C	9 to 30 months	Standardized toys	Bromwich 1981 Department of Educational Psychology, School of Education, California State University
Callier Azusa Scale	Motor, perceptual, daily living, cognition, communication, socialization	C	Birth to 9-0 years	Assesses overall development of children who are deaf, blind, or profoundly handicapped	Stillman 1978 University of Texas at Dallas, Callier Center for Communication Disorders
Carolina Curriculum for Infants and Toddlers with Special Needs	Cognition, communication, social adaptation, fine motor and gross motor skills	C (curriculum embedded)	Birth to 24 months	Assessment log and developmental progress charts that can serve as an evaluation of sorts	Johnson Martin, Jens, Attermeier, & Hacker 1991 Paul H. Brookes Publishing Co.

continued on next page

Appendix 5A

Test Name	Area(s) Assessed	Norm- or Criterion-referenced	Age Range	Notes	Author/Publisher
Communication and Symbolic Behavior Scales	Communication, social-affective, symbolic	N	9 months to 6-0 years	Parent and professional observation	Wetherby & Prizant 2003 Riverside Publishing
Communicative Evaluation Chart	Overall language development	C	3 months to 5-0	Observation, following directions, verbal and motor productions, drawing, answering questions	Anderson, Miles, & Matheny 1963 Educators Publishing Service
Compton-Hutton Phonological Assessment	Phonology	C	Any age	Picture identification	Compton & Hutton 1978 Carousel House
Early Social Communication Scales	Social and communicative competencies of children who have little to no language	C	Birth to 30 months	Caregiver interview, observation	Seibert & Hogan 1981 University of Miami Mailman Center for Child Development
Environmental Language Intervention Program	Expressive grammatical forms and function	N	1-1 to 4-9 years	Conversation, imitation, play	MacDonald 1978 Merrill
Environmental Prelanguage Battery	Pre-linguistic skills (play, imitation, turn taking)	C	1-0 to 2-6	Observation, play, imitation, object identification, picture identification, following directions	Horstmeier & MacDonald 1978 Merrill
Expressive One-Word Picture Vocabulary Test	Expressive vocabulary	N	2-0 to 11-11 years	Uses pictures	Gardner 1979 Academic Therapy Publications
Fluharty Preschool Speech and Language Screening Test	Articulation, receptive and expressive language	N	2-0 to 6-0 years	Object identification, picture identification, sentence repetition	Fluharty 1978 Teaching Resources
Goldman-Fristoe Test of Articulation	Articulation	N	2-0 to 16-0+ years	Picture identification, story retell and imitation	Goldman & Fristoe 1986 American Guidance Service
Hawaii Early Learning Profile (HELP)	Cognitive, expressive language, gross motor skills, fine motor skills, self-help, social-emotional	C	Birth to 36 months	Curriculum embedded	Enrichment Project for Handicapped Infants 1979 VORT Corporation
Hodson Assessment of Phonological Processes	Phonological patterns	C	Any age	Child plays with objects and SLP transcribes word level responses	Hodson 1986 Pro-Ed

continued on next page

Appendix 5A

Test Name	Area(s) Assessed	Norm- or Criterion-referenced	Age Range	Notes	Author/Publisher
Infant Scale of Communicative Intent	Pre-linguistic skills	C	Birth to 1-6 years	Observation	Sacks & Young 1982 St. Christopher's Hospital for Children
Infant-Toddler and Family Instrument	Parent-caregiver interview, developmental map, checklist of concerns about child and family	C	6 to 36 months	Designed to help home visitors organize their impressions of family and child well-being	Apfel & Provence 2001 Paul H. Brookes Publishing Co.
Infant-Toddler Developmental Assessment (includes Provence Birth to Three Developmental Profile)	The Provence section assesses feelings, social adaptation, personality traits, motor, language, and cognitive	C	Birth to 3-0 years	Family-centered assessment process; framework for review and integration of data from multiple sources as well as guidelines for team process and decision-making	Provence, Erikson, Vater, & Palmeri 1995 Riverside
Khan-Lewis Phonological Analysis	Articulation and phonology	C/N	Any age (norms for 1-0 to 5-11 years)	Picture identification from Goldman-Fristoe	Khan & Lewis 1986 American Guidance Service
Language Development Survey: A Screening Tool for Delayed Language Toddlers	Expressive language	C	2 year olds	Parent completed survey form	Rescorla 1989 *Journal of Speech & Hearing Disorders*
Lowe and Costello Symbolic Play Test	Play behaviors	C	1-0 to 3-0 years	Standardized toys	Lowe & Costello 1976 Nelson Publishing
MacArthur Communicative Development Inventories (CDI)	Communication development, particularly grammatical development	C	8 months – 37 months	Parent report	Fenson, Dale, Resnick, Thal, Bates, Hartung, Pethick, & Reilly 1993 Thomson Learning
Observation of Communicative Interaction	Interactions between mother and infant	C	Infants	Observation	Klein & Briggs 1987 *Journal of Childhood Communication Disorders*
Parent/Caregiver Involvement Scale (PCIS)	Maternal behaviors	C	3 months to 3-0 years	Ratings of maternal behaviors from videotaped samples	Farran, Kasari, Comfort, & Jay 1986 Continuing Education, UNC at Greensboro
Peabody Picture Vocabulary Test–Third Edition	Receptive vocabulary	N	2-5 to 40 years	Uses pictures; has to point to 1 of 4	Dunn & Dunn 1997 American Guidance Service

continued on next page

Appendix 5A

Test Name	Area(s) Assessed	Norm- or Criterion-referenced	Age Range	Notes	Author/Publisher
Preschool Language Scale 4 (PLS-4)	Auditory comprehension, verbal expression	N	Birth to 6-11 years	Response to pictures, object manipulation, picture ID, following directions	Zimmerman, Steiner, & Pond 2002 Psychological Corporation
Receptive-Expressive Emergent Language Test–Third Edition (REEL-3)	Pre-linguistic skills	N	Birth to 3-0 years	Parent report	Bzoch, League, & Brown 2003 Pro-Ed
Reynell Developmental Language Scales	General receptive and expressive language skills	N	1-0 to 5-0 years	Observation, picture identification, objective identification, and manipulation	Reynell 1969 NFER Publishers
The Rossetti Infant-Toddler Language Scale: A Measure of Communication and Interaction	Interaction, attachment, play, pragmatics, gesture, comprehension, and expression	C	Birth to 3-0 years	Parent report, elicited behaviors, spontaneously observed behaviors	Rossetti 1990 LinguiSystems, Inc.
Sequenced Inventory of Communication Development–Revised (SICD)	Sound awareness and discrimination, comprehension, motor, vocal, and verbal expression	N	4 months to 4-0 years	Parent report, object manipulation, picture identification, following directions	Hedrick, Prather, & Tobin 1984 Pro-Ed
Transdisciplinary Play-Based Assessment	Cognitive, social-emotional, communication, sensori-motor	C	Birth to 6-0 years	Curriculum-embedded; suitable for arena use	Linder 1990 Paul H. Brookes Publishing Co.
Vineland Social Maturity Scale (Revised)	Communication, daily living skills, socialization, motor	N	Birth to adult	Questionnaire	Doll 1985 American Guidance Service

Symbolic Play Scale Checklist

Appendix 5B

Play	Language

Stage I 9 to 12 months
• Awareness that objects exist when not seen, finds toy hidden under scarf
• Means-end behavior: crawls or walks to get what he wants, pulls string toys
• Does not mouth or bang all toys, some used appropriately
	• No true language; may have performative words (words that are associated with actions or the total situation)
	Exhibits following communicative functions:
	  –request (instrumental)
	  –command (regulatory)

Stage II 13 to 17 months
• Purposeful exploration of toys; discovers operation of toys through trial and error, uses variety of motoric schemas
• Hands toy to adult if unable to operate
	• Context dependent single words (e.g., child may use the word *car* when riding in a car, but not when he sees a car); words tend to come and go in child's vocabulary
	Exhibits following communicative functions:
	  –request –protesting
	  –command –label
	  –interactional –response
	  –personal –greeting

Stage III 17 to 19 months
• Autosymbolic play (e.g., child pretends to go to sleep or pretends to drink from cup or eat from spoon)
• Uses most common objects and toys appropriately
• Tool use (uses stick to reach toy)
• Finds toys invisibly hidden (when placed in box and box emptied under scarf)
	• Beginning of true verbal communication, words have following functional and semantic relations:
	  –recurrence –agent
	  –existence –object
	  –nonexistence –action or state
	  –rejection –location
	  –denial –object or person associated with object or location

Stage IV 19-22 months
• Symbolic play extends beyond the child's self.
• Plays with dolls (e.g., brushes doll's hair, feeds doll a bottle, covers doll with blanket)
• Child performs pretend activities on more than one person or object (e.g., feeds self, a doll, mother, and another child)
• Combines two toys in pretend play (e.g., puts spoon in pan or pours from pot into cup)
	• Refers to objects and persons not present
	• Beginning of word communication with following semantic relations:
	  –agent-action –action-locative
	  –action-object –object-locative
	  –agent-object –possessive
	  –attributive –dative

Stage V 24 months
• Represents daily experience, plays house (e.g., is the mommy, daddy, or baby; objects used are realistic and close to life-size)
• Events short and isolated; no true sequences; some self-limiting sequences (e.g., puts food in pan, stirs, and eats)
• Block play consists of stacking and knocking down
• Sand and water play consist of filling, pouring, and dumping
	• Uses earlier pragmatic functions and semantic relations in phrases and short-sentences
	• The following morphological markers appear:
	  –present progressive (-ing) on verbs
	  –plurals
	  –possessives

Stage VI 2 ½ years
• Represents events less frequently experienced or observed, particularly impressive or traumatic events:
  –doctor-nurse-sick child
  –teacher-child
  –store-shopping
• Events still short and isolated. Realistic props still required. Roles shift quickly.
	• Responds appropriately to the following *wh-* questions in context:
	  –what –who
	  –whose –where
	  –what . . . do
	• Asks *wh-* questions, generally puts *wh-* at beginning of sentence
	• Responds to *why* questions inappropriately except for well-known routines, such as, "Why is the doctor here?" "Baby sick."
	• Asks *Why?*, but often inappropriate and does not attend to answers

Westby, C. (1980). Assessment of cognitive and language abilities through play. *Language, Speech, and Hearing Services in Schools, 3,* 154-168. Reprinted by permission.

Chapter 6

Treatment Methods, Techniques, and Materials

Chapter 2 discussed some of the unique features in service delivery for infants and toddlers. This chapter will address other unique features important for infants and toddlers. You'll find descriptions of different treatment methods, including the philosophy of the methods and information on materials that are useful with this population.

Activity-based Instruction

Infants past the first few months of life need to learn that their actions can result in a change in their environment. Dunst (1981) describes some methods that are appropriate for infants and they are elaborated on by Bricker and Cripe (1992). Bricker and Cripe call their method of intervention *activity-based intervention*. They differentiate activity-based intervention from direct instruction. Direct instruction uses a stimulus-response association and operant conditioning principles. Activity-based intervention, while relying on the appropriate use of behavioral learning principles, employs these in a different manner. An activity-based approach does not teach children to respond to specific cues under specific conditions, but teaches functional skills across development domains mostly in child-initiated activities. This approach is based on the knowledge that young children learn best when they are actively engaged. Some principles of an activity-based framework for intervention include:

- **Guided learning**
  Play situations are arranged so that the situation attracts the infant's attention and is somewhat challenging. The environment (how the task is set up) guides the learning. Perhaps the infant responds to the door chimes that are not in the line of sight. Using guided learning, the parent might present a variety of different kinds of noisemakers (e.g., whistle, clapping hands, music) from many different locations. The situation is enticing to the infant because she is already responding to sounds out of sight, and it is challenging because the sounds are new and are coming from different directions.

- **Violating expectations**
  This technique requires that the infant participate in repetitive, predictable play sequences (e.g., pushing a car back and forth with the adult, pulling a cloth off a hidden toy). The clinician then alters the sequence without warning (e.g., pushes the car off the table; removes the hidden toy so that the next time the cloth is removed, nothing is there). This should surprise the infant and elicit some response, perhaps a vocalization or change in facial expression.

- **Forgetfulness**
  The adult can purposely forget something that is part of a routine (e.g., when dressing the child, put on one shoe and forget to put on the other). The goal is for the child to notice that something is missing and communicate this in some way.

- **Using novelty**
  Rather than having the same toys always available or using the same plate and spoon at mealtimes, introduce something new into the environment. For children who are uncomfortable with change, introduce one novel feature into a familiar routine. Other children may do better when something entirely new is introduced into the environment.

- **Piece by piece**
  This strategy can be used when playing with any toys that have pieces (e.g., puzzles, blocks, crayons). Rather than putting all of the pieces out at one time, the adult holds back some of the pieces and waits for the child to communicate to get more. Bricker and Cripe caution, however, that having the child ask for each piece may destroy the continuity of the activity.

Hart and Risley (1974) describe additional techniques for infants.

- **Sabotage**
  This strategy involves deliberately interfering with the successful completion of the activity. For example, if playing with the toy that has pieces that are meant to be hit with a hammer, the adult would present only the pieces and not the hammer.

- **Incidental teaching**
  This technique builds on what the child can already do, and tries to elicit a more advanced response. For example, perhaps the infant is finding a partially hidden object. When the child is reaching for the toy, cover the toy completely. This should shape a more advanced behavior—finding a completely hidden object. This incidental teaching may be used for older toddlers, and is described below as *following the child's lead*.

A more complete list of different strategies that can be used is found in the *Activities Book*, pages 159–161. It explains the strategies to the parents, but is also helpful to clinicians.

A Partnership Model: Following the Child's Lead

Infants and toddlers are not "designed" to sit and work on structured activities as a 5- or 6-year-old child might. They are constantly exploring their environment and stay with an object or activity for only a short time. This means that going into the session with a structured plan for the five treatment activities you want to complete is probably going to result in frustration for you and the child. Instead, you should begin the session with an idea of the goal(s) and treatment objective(s) you want to accomplish with treatment activities ready for each, but be flexible enough to adapt and follow the child's lead.

Rossetti (2001) reiterates this principle when he states that "Although goal setting is an important part of intervention, the primary purpose is not to finish a planned activity . . . rather the primary purpose is to gain the child as a communicative partner." For example, perhaps you wanted to work on a receptive language treatment objective of understanding the concept of "one" and had prepared an activity with blocks and a sorting toy during which you were going to ask the child to "put in just one." However,

Chapter 6: Treatment Methods, Techniques, and Materials

the child shows no interest in the sorting toy and instead gets out the stacking rings. You could still accomplish your objective but would need to do so using the stacking rings.

At times you will also have to totally switch the objective you had in mind. Maybe the child is not interested in any toys or objects that would work well to teach the concept of *one*, but she gets out her stuffed animals of varying sizes. You quickly adapt to work on another treatment objective (e.g., understanding size words). If the child continues to show interest in the stuffed animals, consider what other treatment objectives might be met (e.g., an expressive language goal to use a two-word phrase).

MacDonald and Carroll (1995) describe following the child's lead as using a partnership model for communicating with infants. They state that adults often fail to see their daily interactions as opportunities to naturally teach the child to communicate. They call this *natural therapy* and describe five important goals for the adult in this interaction.

Adult goals	How to do it
Balance: Act like the child and communicate as much as the child does. Each partner contributes equally to the exchange.	Occasionally physically prompt the child to show how to initiate or take a turn. Initiate contacts but then wait expectantly for the child to take her turn. Give the child time to take her turn. Share the choice of activities with the child. Give the child some control in the interaction.
Match: Act like the child and communicate in ways similar to what the child can do. This provides a feasible model for the child. You can show the child what the next step in the communication would be by adding a sound, word, or phrase.	When a joint activity occurs, keep it going by responding in a meaningful way. Respond to movements with similar movements and occasionally add a sound. Match child's sounds and occasionally add a word. Respond to a word with one or two words. Be childlike in your interactions.
Responsiveness: Respond sensitively and in different ways to the child's emerging communication. Respond to nonverbal and verbal communication.	Respond to the child's interest and pace. Pay more attention to appropriate behaviors and less to immature or disruptive behaviors. Respond to the child's behaviors and actions as if they were communications.
Nondirectiveness: Follow the child's lead and allow her to share in the direction of interaction.	Follow the child's lead. Comment more than asking questions or giving commands. Limit questions to real questions (e.g., asking "Where is the car?" when the car cannot be found rather than asking an artificial question like "What sound does the car make?"). Wait and expect the child to respond. Match the child's language level and ideas. Try to keep the child interacting for more than one turn.
Emotional attachment: Spontaneously reward by interacting with the child for the fun of it rather than for getting something done. This reduces stress.	Actively enjoy the child. Be animated. Show childlike play style. Avoid negative judgments of the child. Concentrate on keeping the interaction going rather than correcting errors in communication.

Effective Consequences

In each of the models described previously (activity-based and partnership), the clinician uses consequences. Johnson-Martin et al. (1991) remind us that a consequence is "merely an act that follows another act as an effect or as a result of the former." Consequences can cause a behavior to occur again or make it less likely to occur again. Using effective consequences means utilizing behavior management techniques.

Swigert (1998) provides a summary of basic behavior management techniques that can be used to increase, decrease, or change behavior.

Techniques used to increase the frequency of a behavior

- Positive reinforcement
  Adds something to the environment that will increase the likelihood behavior will occur again. This might be a verbal reinforcement such as "good talking" or a more tangible reinforcement like a sticker or cookie.

- Negative reinforcement
  Allows the child to get out of a situation she perceives as negative. Perhaps the child does not want to follow directions (perceived as negative) while sitting at the table and would rather be running around. If the child were allowed to get down right away and not follow any commands, this consequence would negatively reinforce her refusal to follow commands. Instead, negative reinforcement could be applied by having the child follow several directions at the table and then letting her get down and run around. This, "getting out of" sitting at the table will reinforce the likelihood that she will follow a few commands the next time.

Techniques used to decrease the frequency of a behavior

- Extinction
  Terminates ongoing reinforcement that has, perhaps unknowingly, been reinforcing a behavior. For example, the goal is to have the child use a manual sign or gesture to indicate what she wants. The child has been grunting and pointing to the toy box so the parents open it and offer the child different toys until they find the one the child wants. By giving the child the toy she wants when she grunts and points, the parents are offering positive reinforcement for this behavior. If they stop this and instead demand that the child imitate a gesture before giving her the toy, they are using extinction to decrease the frequency of grunting and pointing.

- Differential reinforcement of other behavior
  Stops an unwanted behavior and replaces it with an acceptable one. It uses a combination of extinction and positive reinforcement. In the toy box example provided above, if the parents praised the child after she imitated the gesture (positive reinforcement), they would be using differential reinforcement of other behavior because it is paired with extinction.

- Antecedent manipulation
  Changes the course of events immediately prior to an unwanted behavior to decrease the likelihood that the behavior will occur. For example, when working with a child to increase her ability to show the functional use of objects, the caregivers noticed that whenever they included a cup among the objects, the child became fixated on the cup and did not want to give it up and go on to other objects. Using antecedent manipulation, the caregivers chose different objects and did not include the cup.

- Punishment
  The opposite of *reinforcement*. When using punishment, a consequence is provided after the behavior. The consequence is intended to reduce the likelihood that the behavior will occur again. Punishment should be used sparingly, and typically in situations in which the child's safety is in question. For example, a goal might be for the child to respond to the command, "Come here." The child has a tendency to run away from the caregiver and does not return when called. The situation might occur in which the child places herself in danger by failing to respond to the command "Come here." In a situation such as this, the parent might choose to use punishment (e.g., a stern "NO!," quickly picking up the child and placing her in time out).

Techniques to help a child acquire a new behavior

- Prompting
  Giving a verbal instruction, a cue, or a physical assist to help the child achieve the target behavior. For example, when working on sound development, the prompt might involve touching the child's lips or helping her move her tongue to produce the sound.

- Modeling
  Showing the child what you want her to do by first doing it yourself. For example, when developing expressive language, model the word or phrase you want the child to use and then ask her to imitate it.

- Shaping a behavior
  Gradually increasing the level of difficulty of the stimulus to help the child achieve a higher level of complexity. If the child is unable to perform an action or give a response to the full extent that you expect, break the activity into smaller steps. For example, if the activity is to have the child follow a two-step direction (e.g., find the doggie and put him on the chair), but the child can't complete the entire command, you could reinforce each step as it occurs. You could tell the child, "Find the dog" and maybe point to the dog. Then when the child finds the dog, you can say, "Put the dog on the chair" and point to the chair. Once the child can do each part of the direction, put them together for the complete two-step direction.

There are other ways to shape the child's response so she can be successful and you can offer positive reinforcement. See the examples on the next page.

- If the child is expected to select an object named from two or three objects, place the object you're going to name a little closer to the child.

- In sound production, you might first just want the child to put her lips together as she tries to make the /m/ sound. Then you might ask her to put her lips together and make a humming sound.

- In receptive language development, you may be working to help the child learn to identify body parts. At first you might hold the child's hand and help her tap her head when you say, "Show me your head." Then you might simply help the child move her hand close to her head before you give the command. You might finally make it more difficult by simply giving the command without any physical prompting.

> **Making Consequences Effective**
>
> Use naturally-occurring consequences (e.g., giving the child the object she points to).
>
> Social consequences are powerful (e.g., the other children in the classroom interact more with the child as her communication increases).
>
> Different children respond to different consequences.
>
> Consequences must be changed often.
>
> A consequence must immediately follow the behavior.
>
> When the child can understand language, explain the consequence.
>
> Johnson-Martin et al. (1991)

Remediation, Redefinition, and Re-education

The approaches and techniques described thus far have focused on interaction with the child. The intervention principles described above would fall into the remediation category in the schema described by Sameroff and Fiese (1990) and Theadore et al. (1994). These authors remind interventionists that *redefining* and *re-educating* are equally important techniques.

- *Remediation* helps children develop skills that more closely approximate those of their chronological peers.

- *Redefinition* helps caregivers redefine their perception of the child's abilities by helping them evaluate the child's strengths and weaknesses. Redefining does not mean telling the parents that you know best what their child can and cannot do. It **does** mean working carefully with the parents over time to help them form realistic expectations for their child. Sometimes this involves helping parents adjust their sights downward if they have unrealistic expectations for what their child is able to do. For example, the parents want their toddler, who has significant motor impairments, to be able to climb onto the couch. They are frustrated because the child screams when she can't get onto the couch. Climbing onto the couch does not seem to be a realistic expectation for the child, at least in the near future. You might help parents redefine their goal as eliminating the screaming behavior and substituting instead an appropriate communicative behavior when the child wants help to get up on the couch. In other instances you may have to help parents redefine their expectations to a higher level. For example, the parents may think their child is unable to communicate in any way because the child is not saying words. You may need to help parents redefine their idea of communication so they recognize that when the child is using gestures or facial expressions, communication is indeed taking place.

- *Re-education* provides direct instruction to the parents/caregivers to help them better understand their child's developmental needs. Re-education occurs continually during your interactions with the parents. Explain why you are suggesting a specific goal for the child so the parents understand that it is appropriate for their child at this particular developmental age. For example, the mother of a 15-month-old nonverbal child with a tracheostomy was teaching the child signs to communicate but had chosen mostly names of farm animals to teach. Re-education involves explaining why it might be more appropriate to teach more meaningful signs to the child (e.g., eat, more).

Treatment Materials

Older children may be satisfied working with pictures and pages from workbooks in therapy, but for infants and toddlers, the work of therapy must be done in a playful context. That means that the materials for therapy will be toys and objects found in the child's natural environments. Appendix 6A (pages 73–74) lists some favorite toys and materials for this population. Avoid stuffed animals and things that won't wipe clean. When you see a stuffed animal listed, we assume that you are providing services in the child's home and are using her stuffed animal.

Cleaning the toys and materials

Children under the age of three are much more likely to mouth toys, drool on toys, and generally get materials dirty faster than older children on your caseload. An advantage to using the toys the child has at her home is that you don't have to worry about cleaning them before taking them to another home for another child to use. If you are taking toys from place to place, keep a separate plastic bag in your car to deposit any toys mouthed by a child. Don't take that toy into the next child's home. Many toys can be placed in the dishwasher for efficient cleaning. Others can be wiped clean with a disinfectant.

Summary

The treatment methods used with children birth to three have evolved as this area of practice has grown. Effective methods have been found to be child- and family-centered. In addition, it's important to follow the child's lead as much as possible. Applying specific behavioral techniques will help increase desirable behaviors. Using materials that will engage the child will help make treatment more effective.

Suggested Toys, Materials, and Books for Therapy

Appendix 6A

Art Supplies
- coloring book/drawing paper
- crayons, pencils
- empty boxes (shoe box, tissue box)
- empty paper towel rolls
- glue/glue stick
- masking tape
- ribbon
- stickers

Bathroom
- cotton balls
- shampoo
- shaving cream
- soap
- toothbrush
- unbreakable mirror
- washcloth/towel

Clothes
- bib
- dress-up clothes (purses, hats, apron with pocket, etc.)
- shoes
- socks

Kitchen Items
- 2-liter bottles
- bags of various types and sizes (e.g., plastic, paper, shopping)
- dust pan with broom
- empty food boxes/cans
- ice block (Blue Ice)
- measuring cups
- placemats
- plastic bowls, cups, plates, teapot
- play food
- pots and pans
- small, clear plastic containers with lids
- sponge or cleaning rag
- wooden spoons
- zippered plastic bags

Blocks
- Duplo
- Mega Bloks

Dolls/Puppets
- male and female dolls with clothes
- puppets (mouth must open)
- stuffed animals

Puzzles
- M&M color matching puzzle
- puzzles with knobs (animals, common objects)

Furniture/Large Toys
- bed
- chairs
- infant swing
- slide
- stroller
- table (washable)
- TV
- wagon

Noisy Toys
- keys
- musical instruments
- rattles
- any toy that makes noise or moves

Sets
- Fisher Price Loving Family (people and house)
- Little People Animal Sounds Farm
- Mr. Potato Head (ages 2+)
- Pretend & Play Kitchen Set

Stacking/Nesting Toys
- nesting cups
- plastic eggs that open
- stacking rings/blocks

Vehicles (different sizes)
- boat or floating object
- bus (Fisher Price Little People bus)
- cars (some large enough for toy people to fit in)
- fire truck
- police car
- train
- wagon (large enough so toy people/animals will fit in it)

Miscellaneous Items
- beanbag
- bell
- blanket
- books
- bucket
- carpet square
- cloth diapers
- discarded envelopes
- doorbell
- family photos
- flashlight
- handheld fan
- magazines (ads)
- mesh bag
- newspaper
- paper
- pillow and pillowcase
- plastic bottles with childproof lids
- remote control for TV
- shaving cream
- stairs
- tape recorder or radio
- telephone

continued on next page

Appendix 6A

Miscellaneous Toys
- balls (assorted sizes)
- bubbles (in a no-spill container)
- doll bathing materials (fake shampoo, washtub, washcloth, etc.)
- play dough
- pounding toys (Little Tikes Pound Bench, Little Tikes Discover Sounds Tool Box)
- toy telephone

Books
- *Babies* by Gyo Fujikawa
- *Baby's 1, 2, 3* by Neil Ricklen
- *Baby's Colors* by Neil Ricklen
- *Baby's Friends* by Neil Ricklen
- *Baby's Home* by Neil Ricklen
- *Baby's Good Night* by Neil Ricklen
- *Boswell Wide Awake* by Alexandra Day
- *Brown Bear, Brown Bear What Do You See?* by Bill Martin Jr and Eric Carle
- *Carl's Birthday* (board) by Alexandra Day
- *Cat's Play* by Lisa Campbell Ernst
- *Chester's Way* by Kevin Henkes
- *Counting Kisses* by Karen Katz
- *Daddy and Me* by Neil Ricklen
- *D.W.'s Guide to Preschool* by Marc Brown
- *Good Night Gorilla* by Peggy Rathman
- *Here Comes Tabby Cat* by Phyllis Root
- *I Love You Because You're You* by Liza Baker
- *I Spy Little Wheels* (and other *I Spy* board books) by Jean Marzollo and Walter Wick
- *I Used to Be the Baby* by Robin Ballard
- *Is the Spaghetti Ready?* by Frank B. Edwards and John Bianchi
- *Jesse Bear, What Will You Wear?* by Nancy White Carlstrom
- *Jessica* by Kevin Henkes
- *Lovey Dovey* by Mary Englebreit
- *Max Drives Away* by Rosemary Wells
- *Mommy and Me* by Neil Ricklen
- *My First Word Board Book* by Angela Wilkes
- *My Hippie Grandmother* by Reeve Lindbergh
- *My Somebody Special* by Sarah Weeks
- *No Ordinary Olive* by Roberta Baker
- *Ogres! Ogres! Ogres! A Feasting Frenzy from A-Z* by Nicholas Heller
- *On The Town* by Judith Casely
- *Only You* by Rosemary Wells
- *Polar Bear, Polar Bear, What Do You Hear?* by Bill Martin Jr and Eric Carle
- *Sam Loves Kisses* by Yves Got
- *She Did It!* by Jennifer A. Ericsson
- *Show Me!* by Tom Tracy
- *Silly Sally* by Audrey Wood
- *The Big Book of Beautiful Babies* by David Ellwand
- *The Grouchy Ladybug* by Eric Carle
- *The Very Hungry Caterpillar* by Eric Carle
- *There's a Big, Beautiful World Out There* by Nancy Carlson
- *Tickle Tickle* by Dakari Hru
- *What Do Smurfs Do All Day?* by Peyo
- *What Mommies Do Best* by Laura Jolle Numeroff
- *What Shall We Do with the Boo-Hoo Baby?* by Cressida Cowell and Ingrid Godon
- *Where Are You Going? To See My Friends* by Eric Carle and Kazuo Iwamura
- *Where Is Maisy?* by Lucy Cousins
- *Where's Spot?* by Eric Hill
- *Where's Wallace?: Story and Panoramas* by Hillary Knight
- *Who Hoots?* by Katie Davis
- *Who Hops?* by Katie Davis
- *Who Said Moo?* by Harriett Ziefert and Simms Taback
- *Wibbly Pig Likes Bananas* by Mick Inkpen
- books with a variety of realistic, familiar photos
- Touch and Feel Books by DK Publishing

Chapter 7

Intervention for Pre-linguistic Skills

Pre-linguistic behaviors are those that do not involve language. However, this does not mean that communication is not involved. To the contrary, these pre-linguistic behaviors are often quite communicative, or are at least behaviors that are laying the groundwork for the development of later communication skills. A potpourri of skills that lay the groundwork for later communication include attention, interaction, attachment, cognitive, social-emotional, problem solving, and play. Interaction, in particular, often involves early pre-linguistic communication.

It is important to target pre-linguistic skills, as the child will derive more benefit from later linguistic intervention (Rossetti 2001). Yoder and Warren (1993) suggest two main reasons to target pre-linguistic development:

1. Enhancing the child's intentional communication and vocalization lays a foundation for better use of adult input in the language development process.

2. As the child's communication attempts become more frequent and more effective, better turn taking between the child and adult is seen.

Principles of Pre-linguistic Intervention

Rossetti (2001) summarizes some principles of pre-linguistic intervention:

Contingent imitation
Imitation skills are very important for the development of other cognitive skills. In contingent imitation, the adult imitates behaviors demonstrated by the child. Prior to five to seven months of age, the child is the primary initiator of communicative interactions. The benefits of contingent imitation include:

- allowing the child to regulate the amount of social stimulation

- encouraging the child to imitate the adult

- causing the child to pay greater attention to the adult

- producing a variety of types of play activities (e.g., vocal play, banging toys, facial expressions, clapping)

Since children up to the ages of about seven months are more interested in faces and objects, this imitation will likely involve face-to-face interaction. Typically the child imitates behaviors he is already using, and then reaches a stage where he will imitate novel behaviors. Imitating novel behaviors usually occurs between 8 and 12 months. Between 12 and 18 months of age, the child will even defer imitations until a later time (Linder 1990).

Chapter 7: Intervention for Pre-linguistic Skills

Contingent responsivity
This involves allowing the child to select an object or activity he's interested in and then interacting with the child with that object or activity. The child is better able to maintain attention toward this activity than one that an adult selects.

Scaffolding
This involves building on or adding to the child's communicative attempt. The adult gives a prompt for the child to respond in a more mature way to communicate the same message. For example, if the child pushes the spoon away when he does not want another bite, the adult might prompt the child to use the manual sign for "stop" or a head shake for "no" as a more mature way to communicate that message.

Using social routines
Routines are turn-taking rituals that occur in a predictable way during the child's day. It might be a game such as "peek-a-boo" or a routine that occurs at bath time every day. Families of children developing typically use many routine games throughout the day. However families of children with special needs may be so occupied caring for those needs that they do not have time to develop such verbal rituals without specifically being taught. Since these routines are highly repetitive and predictable, it helps the child learn what the appropriate interaction is during the ritual.

Attachment

Social-emotional development is largely tied to the *attachment* that forms between the mother and the child. *Attachment* has been defined as a unique relationship between two people that lasts over time (Klaus & Kennell 1976). When there is not a mother-child bond, or attachment, there may be later caregiving deficiencies.

Three major patterns of mother-child attachment have been described (Ainsworth et al. 1978):

- Avoidant
  Infant avoids the caregiver by failing to give a greeting, playing with his back to the caregiver, and avoiding eye contact.

- Secure
  Infant greets the caregiver promptly and seeks out the caregiver. He uses the caregiver as a base to explore his environment. When distressed, a secure infant is easily soothed.

- Resistant
  Infant is noted for repeated expressions of anger, crying, whining, etc. These behaviors are most apparent during reunion situations. When distressed, resistant infants are hard to soothe or console.

Interaction Skills

Social-emotional stability influences the development of *interaction* skills such as turn taking and ability to initiate interaction. These reciprocal interactions are important factors in the child's development. Infants interact with adults through actions such as eye contact, crying, quieting, paying attention to faces and voices, and body movements. If the caregiver and the infant are able to synchronize these behaviors and responses, there is a long-term positive effect on cognitive, social, and linguistic skills (Sparks et al. 1988). Something as simple as the mother talking to her child can have a significant impact on the child's development. For example, mothers who do not frequently talk to their premature infants have children who score lower on developmental scales than children who received adequate interaction from their mothers (Jacobsen et al. 1988).

You can help these interactions develop between the child and the caregiver. When the child is not able to reinforce the interactions of the caregiver (e.g., doesn't laugh, can't take turns), the caregiver is less motivated to continue interacting with the child. You may have to help the caregiver adapt her interactions (e.g., give the child longer to respond). Once the child reaches 12–24 months of age, he needs to begin to initiate the social interactions, not only with his caregivers, but with a broader range of peers and adults (Johnson-Martin et al. 1991).

Attention

Attention is important to the development of interaction skills. When considering the development of *attention* in the birth-to-three age range, we are not really talking about attention span. We are talking about the child's ability to notice and then attend briefly to things and people in his environment. Children will find different kinds of stimuli to be of varying levels of interest. Some children need more external reinforcement to maintain their attention.

Problem-solving Skills

Problem-solving skills are also important to later receptive and expressive language development. Problem solving begins in infancy when the child learns that his behaviors (e.g., crying) can affect a predictable change in the environment. Being successful at problem solving helps the child remain motivated to learn and begins development of cause and effect. Successful problem solving relies on the development of cognitive skills such as object permanence, means-end behavior, functional use of objects, and object classification.

It may be difficult for children with significant motor impairments to perform actions and behaviors that cause a desired result (e.g., pushing the keys on a musical toy). In these instances, modifications will have to be made to help the child develop problem-solving skills (Johnson-Martin et al. 1991).

Pragmatics/Communicative Intent

A child's pre-linguistic communication can be classified by the communicative intent/pragmatic function just as verbal expression can. A child may use behaviors such as eye gaze, reaching, crying, pointing, and gesturing to indicate an intent to:

- answer

- acknowledge

Chapter 7: Intervention for Pre-linguistic Skills

- seek attention

- comment on an object or action

- request objects, actions, or information

- protest

- greet

An awareness of these functions and the ages at which they typically appear will be helpful in planning intervention.

Pre-linguistic Behaviors Used to Indicate Communicative Intent

Communicative Intent	Age (in months)	Pre-linguistic Behaviors
Answer	9-18	Points to Mommy when asked "Where's Mommy?"
Acknowledge	9-18	Looks at speaker
Seek attention	12-18	Cries or touches parent on the hand
Comment on action	12-18	Vocalizes when someone pushes his swing
Comment on object	13-17	Holds up empty bottle to adult
Request objects	13-17	Points to what he wants
Request actions	13-17	Rocks forward in the swing to indicate he wants the swing pushed
Protest	13-17	Screams when parent attempts to cut fingernails
Greet	13-17	Waves bye-bye
Request information	24	Touches a closed box and vocalizes with rising intonation to inquire what's inside

Caregivers often attribute a *communicative intent* to a child's action that may not have been intended. For example, a child may hit the tray on his high chair with his hand while the mother is putting more food on the spoon. The child's mother may interpret this as the child telling her to hurry up with the next bite. There may not have been any communicative intent on the child's part. However, if the mother responds as if there were, the child may begin to use that gesture in a meaningful way.

Chapter 7: Intervention for Pre-linguistic Skills

Play

The importance of analyzing the child's ability to *play* cannot be overemphasized. Early play behaviors relate to the development of communication skills, and can yield some information about the child's overall development. Therefore, developing appropriate play skills is an important precursor to the development of communication skills. Linder (1990) summarizes categories of play that the child exhibits as cognitive skills develop:

- Exploratory or sensori-motor play
  This is an activity done just for the enjoyment or physical sensation (e.g., sound play, banging objects).

- Relational play
  Child uses objects in play for the purposes they were intended (e.g., brushing hair, turning crank on toy). This can be observed in children nine months and older.

- Constructive play
  Child uses objects to construct something with an end in sight (e.g., building with blocks). This is not seen predominantly in children before they are three.

- Dramatic play
  Child pretends to do something or be someone. This can be done with or without objects. This is also called *symbolic play* (e.g., pretends to feed the stuffed animals). Generally seen after two years of age.

- Games with rules play
  The game has preset rules each player knows, even if the rules are made up by the child (e.g., Hide-and-Seek). This is not usually seen in children under three.

- Rough and tumble play
  This is physical play that can be done alone (e.g., hopping) or in a group. This is not typically seen in children under three.

Summary

Intervention designed to improve pre-linguistic skills has three main goals (Rossetti 2001):

- increases the number of enjoyable and successful interactions between the child and the adult

- increases the child's communicative attempts either with or without prompting

- teaches the child how important it is to respond to adult communication attempts

The activities in the *Activities Book* on pages 10–42 should help address the goals on the next page. The activities correspond to the treatment objectives listed in the chart on pages 82–83 (also listed in the *Activities Book* on pages 8–9).

Chapter 7: Intervention for Pre-linguistic Skills

Long-term and Short-term Goals for Pre-linguistic Behaviors

Long-term goal
The child will be able to maintain attention to stimuli and interact with objects and people appropriately.

Short-term goals

PG1 The child will make and maintain eye contact/visual contact with object/picture/person.

PG2 The child will imitate non-vocal actions.

PG3 The child will imitate vocalizations.

PG4 The child will utilize objects (or imaginary objects) in appropriate play/self-care.

PG5 The child will engage in turn-taking routines.

PG6 The child will demonstrate object permanence.

PG7 The child will respond with appropriate gesture/action to sound/speech and/or gesture.

PG8 The child will initiate use of appropriate gesture to obtain desired effect.

PG9 The child will demonstrate other problem-solving skills.

> Note: In order to help narrow your choices of goals, we have provided some suggestions for when to select certain goals. If you follow these suggestions, the goals will match the treatment objectives/activities below and on page 81.

PG1 The child will make and maintain eye contact/visual contact with object/picture/person.

Select when this is the only goal for the activity. Higher-level goals (e.g., using objects appropriately in play) certainly require that the child maintain eye contact with the toy, but it seems unnecessary and irrelevant to list this goal for such an activity.

PG2 The child will imitate non-vocal actions.

Select only when imitation is the goal, not when it is used as a prompt. For example, treatment objective P8 (see page 82) is "imitates facial expressions with adult." Imitation itself is the goal, so that goal is matched to this objective. However, you will find imitation used as a prompt on many activities. For example, activities for P11 (see page 82) [hits objects when playing] use imitation as a method of getting the child to hit the object, but the real goal (the listed goal) is for the child to "utilize objects in appropriate play."

Chapter 7: Intervention for Pre-linguistic Skills

PG3 The child will imitate vocalizations.

The same logic is used as for imitation of non-vocal actions. This goal should be selected as an objective only when imitation itself is the objective (e.g., P7–vocalizes when adult starts vocalization).

PG4 The child will utilize objects (or imaginary objects) in appropriate play/self-care.

Select any time the primary objective is for the child to use real or imaginary objects in play (e.g., P26–imitates stirring with spoon, P29–drops object systematically). Do not use this objective when the object is secondary to the main objective (e.g., P34 [maintains attention to pictures] as the book is secondary, P35 [hands toy back to adult] as the objective is not really playing with the toy but being able to release it).

PG5 The child will engage in turn-taking routines.

Select whenever the adult and child are engaged in an activity that requires taking turns (e.g., P18–cooperates by playing games with adults, P23–plays peek-a-boo, P39–plays ball with adult). Do not select this when the adult and child are doing something together but no turns are required (e.g., P20–imitation of facial expression, P42–imitates doing housework) because the adult and child are doing the activity together, not taking turns).

PG6 The child will demonstrate object permanence.

Select when child is demonstrating (or beginning to demonstrate) understanding that objects exist when they are no longer visible.

PG7 The child will respond with appropriate gesture/action to sound/speech and/or gesture.

Select when child gestures or points in response to the adult's action or gesture (e.g., P17–anticipates what will happen next, P24–waves "Hi" and "Bye", P35–hands toy back to adult). This is not selected when the child is imitating. It is used when the child is responding without the model. Imitation may be used during the activity as a prompt but is not the goal.

PG8 The child will initiate use of appropriate gesture to obtain desired effect.

Select when child is initiating the gesture/action to achieve desired result (e.g., P27–extends toy to show others but doesn't give it up, P38–requests assistance from adult).

PG9 The child will demonstrate other problem-solving skills.

PG6 addresses the development of one problem-solving skill: object permanence. PG9 goal is selected when another problem-solving skill is involved (e.g., P28–overcomes obstacle to obtain object, P40–puts one object inside another).

Chapter 7: Intervention for Pre-linguistic Skills

> **An explanation of how these goals were matched to the treatment activities**
>
> In addition to selecting goals and treatment objectives based on the child's level of function and when the skill is expected to develop, keep in mind the specific communicative intentions that should be developing at the pre-linguistic stage. These are summarized on page 78.
>
> Most treatment objectives (and activities) have only one goal, but some have two (e.g., Treatment Objective P55 [matches shapes] is correlated to PG7 [responding appropriately] and PG9 [other problemsolving]). Keep in mind that additional goals can often be selected for an activity (e.g., turn taking can be matched to many activities such as playing games, playing "peek-a-boo," or playing ball). Some of our distinctions are arbitrary and you might assign goals differently.

Pre-linguistic Ages of Acquisition/Treatment Objectives

Expected age of development	Short-term goal (PG)	Treatment Objectives	Activities to help achieve treatment objectives*
0–3 months	1	Child makes eye contact with adult	P1
	1	Reacts to disappearance of slowly-moving object	P2
	7	Alerts to sound	P3 a, b
	1	Watches speaker's mouth	P4
3–6 months	1	Maintains eye contact	P5
	7	Turns head to voice	P6 a, b
	3	Vocalizes when adult starts vocalization	P7 a, b
	2	Imitates facial expressions with adult	P8
	7	Enjoys repeating newly-learned activity	P9
	8	Reaches for objects	P10
	8	Hits objects when playing	P11 a, b
	6	Finds a partially-hidden object	P12
6–9 months	2	Imitates gestures with adult	P13 a, b
	1	Maintains attention to a speaker	P14
	7	Responds to noisemaker that is not in line of vision	P15
	1	Attends to pictures	P16 a, b
	7	Anticipates what will happen next (e.g., closes eyes, tenses body)	P17 a, b
	5	Cooperates by playing games with adults	P18
	8	Touches toy or adult's hand to restart an activity	P19 a, b
	2	Tries to imitate facial expressions (e.g., puckers, protrudes tongue)	P20
	6	Searches for hidden objects	P21 a, b
	6, 9	Relates sound to object	P22 a, b

*See pages 10–42 in the *Activities Book*.

Chapter 7: Intervention for Pre-linguistic Skills

Expected age of development	Short-term goal (PG)	Treatment Objectives	Activities to help achieve treatment objectives*
9–12 months	5, 6	Plays "Peek-a-boo" by covering and uncovering face with hands or cloth	P23
	7	Waves "Hi" and "Bye"	P24
	8	Points to an object to indicate he knows it is there	P25
	4	Stirs with a spoon	P26
	8	Extends toy to show others but doesn't give it up	P27
	9	Overcomes obstacle to obtain object	P28 a, b
	4	Drops object systematically	P29 a, b
12–15 months	5	Initiates turn-taking routines	P30 a, b
	4	Combs or brushes hair	P31
	4, 7	Hugs dolls, stuffed animals, or people	P32 a, b
	4	Shows functional use of objects	P33 a, b
	1	Maintains attention to pictures	P34
	7	Hands toy back to adult	P35 a, b
15–18 months	4	Uses more than one object in play routine	P36
	4	Pretends action with object	P37 a, b
	8	Requests assistance from adult	P38 a, b, c, d, e
	5	Plays ball with adult	P39
	4, 9	Puts one object inside another	P40 a, b
	7, 9	Identifies self in mirror	P41
	4	Imitates doing housework	P42 a, b, c
18–21 months	4	Pretends to play musical instrument	P43
	3	Imitates environmental noises	P44
	4	Uses two toys together in pretend play	P45 a, b
	7	Pretends to dance	P46 a, b
21–24 months	4	If mobile, pushes a stroller or shopping cart	P47
	4	Flies a toy airplane	P48
	4, 9	Stacks and assembles toys and objects (e.g., nesting blocks)	P49 a, b
	4, 9	Sorts objects	P50 a, b
	7, 9	Matches sounds to pictures of animals	P51
24–27 months	4	Pretends to write	P52
	4	Pretends to talk on the phone	P53
	7	Slaps adult's hand when asked to "Gimme Five"	P54
27–30 months	7, 9	Matches shapes of toys (e.g., square, circle)	P55 a, b, c, d
	7, 9	Matches colors	P56
	4	Dramatizes using doll	P57 a, b
30–33 months	7, 9	Sorts shapes	P58
	7, 9	Stacks rings in correct order	P59
33–36 months	4	Plays house	P60 a, b, c
	7, 9	Sorts colors	P61

*See pages 10–42 in the *Activities Book*.

Therapy Guide
The Early Intervention Kit

Chapter 8

Intervention for Receptive Language

Work on language comprehension occurs in tandem with the work on pre-linguistic skills. For example, if the caregiver and child are playing a game of "peek-a-boo" (a pre-linguistic treatment objective), the adult is using phrases like "Where's baby?" and "There she is." The caregiver is, of course, using language whenever working on pre-linguistic skills with the child, but makes a more concerted effort to assure that the child is understanding language when addressing receptive language goals.

Receptive Skills and Cognitive Development

Receptive language development is tied closely to the development of specific cognitive abilities. For example, a child must understand concepts such as *manner*, *time*, and *cause of events* before she can respond to *what*, *where*, and *who* questions (Piaget 1926). Children sometimes respond to one word they understand in a question (e.g., If the child is asked, "Where do you want to play?," she may respond to the word *play* with the response "baby doll," indicating she didn't really understand that it was a "where" question). The box below shows the typical sequence of when children understand certain question forms.

> **Sequence of Question Comprehension**
>
> *yes/no*
> 1. Rising intonation at the end of the declarative sentence
> 2. Reversing the subject of sentence and the auxiliary verb (e.g., Is Daddy sleeping?)
>
> *wh-* questions
> 1. Inverting subject and auxiliary as well as correctly placing the *wh-* word at the beginning
> 2. *what, where, who* acquired first
> 3. *when, how, why* acquired later
>
> Ervin-Tripp 1970, Tyack & Ingram 1977

Other examples of language comprehension skills that are tied closely to the cognitive development of the child include her understanding of temporal terms, relational terms, and location terms.

Verifying Comprehension

Can you assume that once a child is using a word or phrase she understands it? Receptive language development generally precedes expressive language development. However, a number of children have been reported to produce some words and phrases before they comprehend them (Chapman & Miller 1975, de Villiers & de Villiers 1973). Therefore it is important to verify comprehension of words and phrases the child uses.

When verifying that the child understands a particular word or phrase, it is important to ensure the child is responding to the language and not to other contextual cues. For example, when the child is getting dressed and is asked to "put your arm in here" while the sleeve of the coat is held up for her, there is no way to tell if the child is responding to the verbal direction or to the coat being held up. Verifying comprehension can occur by checking comprehension in multiple contexts or in novel/unusual situations. Using multiple contexts means that you ask the child to put other things "in" before assuming that she really understands the target word. For example, you might ask her to put her feet *in* her shoes, the juice *in* the refrigerator, and the toys *in* the box. However, since these situations all provide contextual cues, you might try a novel or unusual situation. This would involve asking the child to put something in a place it doesn't usually go (e.g., ask the child to put the shoe in the refrigerator).

Strategies to Develop Receptive Language

Receptive language development occurs best in natural contexts throughout the child's day. You can model these strategies and should teach the caregivers these and other strategies to be used in daily activities.

- Labeling
  Consistently label things in the child's environment, especially during daily routines. This allows the child to hear a word over and over again in a familiar context. Those same labels should also be used in new contexts. For instance, if the caregiver says "shoe" each time the child is dressed, the word may become known to the child in relation to her own shoe. It is important that the word also be used to label Mom's shoe, Dad's shoe, the shoe at the store, etc.

- Imitation
  Imitation is an important skill for the child in developing receptive language skills. Imitation seems to be important for the acquisition of words, morphology, and syntactic-semantic structures. As language becomes more complex after age two, imitation seems to be used less as a strategy for language learning. The caregiver can also model correct responses to requests and questions so the child can imitate. For example, if the child is asked to "Put the toys in the box" and she doesn't seem to understand, the caregiver can model the action of picking up the toys. This helps the child learn the meaning of the phrase.

- Focused stimulation
  This can be used to facilitate comprehension (as well as language production). It involves modeling many uses of the target language form. The clinician or the caregiver has to structure the environment so that it is natural and also necessary to use the targeted word (Chapman & Terrell 1994). This technique works well when following the child's lead, as it is not necessary for you to adhere to a rigid protocol. For example, while the child is getting dressed, the caregiver can find multiple opportunities to use words like *shoes, socks, put on, clean*, etc.

Chapter 8: Intervention for Receptive Language

- Modeling
  Show or say what you want the child to do before you expect her to do it. For example, if you are trying to get the child to follow a command to give the baby a kiss, give the baby a kiss first, using language to describe what you are doing.

- Self-talk
  A technique that the caregiver can easily use while completing daily activities is self-talk, a running commentary about the speaker's actions. For example, when the caregiver is cooking dinner, he can use language appropriate to the child's level of comprehension (e.g., single words, phrases, sentences) to describe the actions. If the child understands single words only, the father might say words like *cheese, cut,* or *cook*. If the child understands sentence length utterances, the father might say sentences like, "I'm getting out the cheese," "I'm cutting a piece of cheese," or "I'm cooking the soup."

- Parallel talk
  This is a running commentary about the child's actions. Describe each thing the child does using language at the level the child can understand. For example, if the child is playing with blocks, describe each action: "Quinta is putting the big block on top. The big block fell off. Oh no, all the blocks fell down."

- Supplementing verbal speech with gestures
  To help the child understand what is being said, encourage the use of gestures and/or pointing to accompany speech. For example, if the caregiver is asking the child if she wants to go outside, the caregiver might point to the back door as she says it.

- Supplementing verbal speech with picture stimuli
  To help the child understand what is being said, use pictures to supplement what you are talking about. For example, if you are asking the child if she wants something to eat, show her pictures of her choices (e.g., cheese, apple) as you name them.

- Guided learning
  This strategy involves arranging the environment so something will attract the child's attention and make it somewhat challenging. Perhaps the child is beginning to understand the preposition *under* and can get under the chair when you ask her to. You might ask the child to put the bear under the chair.

- Paraphrasing
  If the child does not seem to have understood what was said, try putting it in other words. For example, if you ask the child to "Give the car a push" and she gives no response, paraphrase to "Make the car go."

The activities described in the *Activities Book* on pages 45–72 should help address the goals on the next page. The activities correspond to the treatment objectives listed in the chart on pages 87–88 (also listed in the *Activities Book* on pages 43–44).

Long-term and Short-term Goals for Receptive Language

Long-term goal

The child will exhibit optimal receptive language skills.

Short-term goals

RG1 The child will respond to speech.

RG2 The child will understand single words from a variety of word classes.

RG3 The child will follow simple one-step commands accompanied by gestures/context clues.

RG4 The child will follow simple one-step commands without gesture/context support.

RG5 The child will follow two- and three-step commands.

RG6 The child will understand simple questions.

Receptive Ages of Acquisition/Treatment Objectives

Expected age of development	Short-term goal (RG)	Treatment Objectives	Activities to help achieve treatment objectives*
3–6 months	1	Recognizes own name	R1
	2	Responds to "no" about half the time	R2
	1	Smiles in response to pleasant speech	R3
6–9 months	2	Responds to "no" most of the time	R4
	2	Moves toward or searches for named family member	R5
	3	Responds to request to "Come here"	R6
9–12 months	2	Gives object in response to verbal request	R7
	4	Performs a routine activity in response to verbal request	R8
	4	Gestures in response to verbal request (e.g., "Wanna come up?")	R9 a, b
	4	Verbalizes or vocalizes in response to verbal request	R10 a, b
	3	Participates in speech routine games (e.g., "So big")	R11
	2, 4	Identifies two body parts on self or doll	R12
	2	Understands some action words	R13 a, b
12–15 months	4	Follows one-step commands during play	R14 a, b
	2, 4	May give kiss on request	R15
	2, 4	Responds to "Give me" while holding object	R16
	2, 6	Points to two action words in pictures	R17
	2, 4	Understands some prepositions	R18
	2, 4	Identifies three body parts on self or doll	R19

*See pages 45–72 in the *Activities Book*.

Chapter 8: Intervention for Receptive Language

Expected age of development	Short-term goal (RG)	Treatment Objectives	Activities to help achieve treatment objectives*
15–18 months	2, 4	Identifies six body parts or clothing items on doll	R20
	2, 4	Show or points to an object on request	R21
	2, 4	Finds familiar objects not in sight	R22
	2, 4	Completes two separate one-step requests with one object	R23
	2, 4	Chooses two familiar objects upon request	R24
	2, 4	Identifies object by category	R25
	2, 6	Finds "baby" in picture	R26
	2	Understands 50 words	R27
18–21 months	2, 4	Identifies four body parts and clothing items on self	R28
	3	Follows commands to "Sit down," "Come here," or "Give me" with gesture	R29
	2, 6	Chooses five familiar objects on request	R30
	2	Understands meaning of action words	R31
	2, 4	Understands words for absent objects by locating them	R32
	2, 4	Identifies pictures when named	R33
	2, 4	Demonstrates some understanding of personal pronouns (e.g., "Give it to her.")	R34 a, b
21–24 months	4	Puts away toy on request	R35
	2, 4	Chooses one object from a group of five on verbal request	R36
	2, 4	Identifies body parts on caregiver or doll	R37
	5	Follows two-step related command	R38
24–27 months	2, 4	Points to four action words in pictures	R39
	2, 4	Understands concept of *one*	R40
	2, 4	Understands size concepts	R41
	2, 4	Points to three or more small body parts on self or caregiver	R42
27–30 months	6	Responds to simple questions	R43
	2, 6	Identifies clothing on self or caregiver	R44
	2, 4	Understands prepositions *on, in, under, out of*	R45
30–33 months	2, 4	Understands five common action words	R46
	5	Follows two-step unrelated commands	R47 a, b
	2, 4	Understands concepts of *one* and *all*	R48
	6	Answers *yes/no* questions correctly	R49 a, b
	6	Understands function of objects	R50
	2, 4	Understands *big* and *little*	R51 a, b
33–36 months	5	Follows three-step unrelated command	R52
	6	Responds to *wh-* questions	R53 a, b, c
	4	Identifies parts of an object	R54 a, b

*See pages 45–72 in the *Activities Book*.

Chapter 9

Intervention for Expressive Language

Expressive language is one of the most visible areas to address. That is, it is easy to judge if the child is making progress just by listening to the child's output. Work on expressive language is tied closely to the development of receptive language skills. In addition, if the child has deficits in sound production/phonology, those goals should be interfaced with expressive language goals.

There are many aspects of expressive language that need to be considered when planning intervention. These aspects overlap, and are not linear, which makes it challenging to keep all of the aspects in mind. The aspects to consider include:

- Communicative Intent of the Message
  Also called *pragmatics*, communicative intent can be expressed with gestures, vocalizations, single words, and word combinations. These communicative intents were indicated on some of the activities in the pre-linguistic chapter to reflect the use of gestures to convey a message.

- Communicative Function Served by the Word Used
  This involves selecting vocabulary to ensure that the child can express a variety of functions. The words should be substantive (mostly nouns, names for things) and relational (words that talk about the relations between objects). You should not, for example, teach only names of objects as this limits the messages the child can send.

- Semantic-Syntactic Relations
  This is observed as two-word utterances emerge. The child is expressing a specific meaning (i.e., semantics) through word order.

- Morphemes
  The child begins to add early morphemic endings (e.g., *-ing, -s*). The morphemes may be used on single words (e.g., runn*ing*, boot*s*).

- Early Sentence Forms
  The development of morphemes allows the child to begin to use early sentence forms. These sentence forms allow him to use structure (form) to express meaning. For example, the child can't use a present progressive sentence form (e.g., "I'm running) until he uses the morpheme *–ing*.

Chapter 9: Intervention for Expressive Language

Communicative Intent of the Message

Using language to control the environment

The earliest forms of expressive language develop in infants and young children as they learn that their nonverbal behaviors and vocalizations can have an impact on their environment. For example, the child learns that when he cries, he receives attention and is picked up and comforted. The child may also learn that by banging on his crib, he calls someone to the room. Noonan and McCormick (1993) summarizes five phases in the development of these environmental control skills:

- Attentional interactions
  These indicate that the child is aware of, recognizes, and anticipates persons, objects, or events.

- Contingency interactions
  The child uses these behaviors to keep an interaction going. For instance, the child might play "peek-a-boo" in order to keep an adult interacting.

- Differentiated interactions
  The child learns to control another person's behavior with a response that has a commonly recognized meaning, such as pointing.

- Encoded interactions
  These are behaviors that have precise meanings and are understood in the situation. They might involve the child using a phrase that is understandable in the situation but not understandable outside the situation. For example, the child might say, "Cat, daddy" as a cat walks into the room and the child wants to point it out to his father.

- Symbolic interactions
  These behaviors can be understood without specific contextual/situational information. For example, the child could say, "Get cookie" and this would be understood regardless of the context.

Pragmatic function of utterances

After the child begins to demonstrate environmental control skills, the next goals should be to further develop word functions, vocabulary, and sentence structure (McCormick & Schiefelbusch 1990). Developing the child's word functions means developing the child's pragmatic skills. These pragmatic functions will be exhibited at the single word and multi-word stage. Examples are provided in the chart on the next page (Coggins & Carpenter 1981, Roth & Spekman 1984, Linder 1990).

Communicative Intent/Pragmatic Function	Age First Seen (in months)	How Expressed at Single Word Stage	How Expressed at Multi-word Stage
Answer	9-18	Says "milk" when asked what he wants	Says "more milk"
Acknowledge	9-18	Says "Gramma" when he hears parents talking about Grandma; can also be repetition of last word heard	Says "my gramma"
Seek/call attention	12-18	Says "Dada"	Says "See that"
Comment on action	12-18	Says "go" when pushed in the swing	Says "Sadie go"
Comment on object	13-17	Says "doggie" while holding toy dog	Says "my doggie"
Request objects	13-17	Says "cookie"	Says "want cookie"
Request actions	13-17	Says "go" while standing by door	Says "wanna go"
Protest	13-17	Says "no" when told it's bedtime	Says "no night-night"
Greeting	13-17	Says "bye"	Says "bye Daddy"
Practicing/repeating	18-24	Repeats words or sounds for practice	Repeats phrases for practice
Request information	24	Says "that?" while pointing to box	Says "What's that?"

When selecting treatment objectives, map them onto the communicative intent of the child (pragmatic use of the communication). That is, it is important to be attuned to the reason for each of the child's communicative behaviors so that pragmatic functions the child is **not** exhibiting can be stimulated. For example, at the 12- to 15-month level, there is an objective that the child will say 8–10 words spontaneously. Consulting the chart above, it is clear that between the ages of 13 and 17 months, the child who is at the one-word stage of expression should begin to use those words to: request an object, request an action, protest, comment on an object or action, greet, and even answer questions. Therefore, it is important when developing the 8–10 words that vocabulary words be chosen that serve those functions and that situations be manipulated to stimulate the word(s) being used in that function. If the child is still primarily in the pre-linguistic stage, one would expect to see those pragmatic functions demonstrated in nonverbal ways. (See box, page 78.)

One other consideration when monitoring development of communicative intentions is the frequency of use. Paul (1995) indicates that 18-month-old children should produce about two instances of intentional communication per minute. By the time the child is 24 months of age, this frequency should increase to five per minute. Paul indicates that the frequency can tell a lot about how motivated the child is to communicate. The form in Appendix 9A (page 106) might prove useful to track the development of these communicative intents.

Communicative Function Served by the Word Used

Choosing expressive language targets

How do you choose which words to teach a young child first? When choosing words to teach, select words that are communicatively useful and have the potential for being combined with other words. It is also a good idea to choose words that can serve a number of communicative functions (e.g., commenting, requesting). Consider choosing words that might occur more frequently in the vocabulary of normally-developing peers (Holland 1975, Lahey & Bloom 1977). You might choose words that are related to ideas and interests the child already has (MacDonald 1989). Additionally, think about the phonological characteristics of the word. How easy or hard will it be for the child to pronounce? Perhaps the child's favorite food is chocolate pudding but the child cannot produce the /ch/ sound. Maybe the child could be taught to use the word *pudding* or an approximation "puh ee" to match his phonological skills.

Holland's core lexicon provides an example for selecting words from which the child's individual lexicon can be built. Some words Holland suggests are:

all gone	no
ball	you
big	your
block	angry words (e.g., *poo, ick, No!*)
car	child's own name
Hi	favorite activity/toy
me	favorite food
more	least favorite food
my/mine	names of significant others

Bloom (1973) dichotomized words as *substantive* (refer to a particular object or to categories of objects) or *relational* (refer to a relationship between objects and include parts of speech such as verbs, adjectives, and prepositions). Nelson (1973) found that about half of the first words used by normally-developing children are nouns. These might be names for important people, names of objects the child interacts with, and labels for objects that move and change (Owens 1992).

Keep in mind that in addition to teaching nouns, you must also teach relational words. Relational words chosen may not always be the most obvious (e.g., *big, hot*), but those that are the most useful to the child. For example, a child with sensory problems who does not like to feel sticky things on his hands may need to be able to comment on sticky things (e.g., "Yuck!") more than he needs to be able to use a relational word such as *big*.

Chapman and Terrell (1994) describe relational words as *action* words and *action-related* words. *Action* words are terms that eventually become true verbs, and *action-related* words are words that are not considered verbs in the adult lexicon, but are used by young children to denote an action (e.g., *in* when putting an object into another or *off* when taking an object off something). When choosing action words, select words appropriate to the child's developmental level.

Remember that children first produce action words to describe their own actions and then they may extend this to include other people performing the actions or objects affected by the action. Therefore, involve the child in movement as much as possible to teach action words.

Chapman and Terrell summarize categories of action-related words that are early to develop:

Category	Examples of Words
Protoverb: Used as a verb; usage often highly ritualistic and tied to the action scheme	*up, in, off, down, no, on here, inside, there, get down, bye-bye, night-night, out, rock-rock, giddy-up, all done, boo*
General purpose words: Do not define a specific action; meaning can be determined only by the context	*do, make*
Deictic words: Used for calling attention to something	*see, there, that*
Object-related action-specific words: An action word used only with respect to an object	*drink, close, open, kick, eat, wash, throw, drop, shake, push, pull, give, get, tear, gimme, wanna, read, kiss*
Intransitive action-specific words: The actions are not object related	*run, walk, hug, dance, fall, sit, jump, stand, cry, get down, stop it, help, come, go*

Appendix 9B (pages 107–108) provides a cross reference of Holland's first lexicon and Chapman and Terrell's relational words to the activities. If you want to work on development of a particular word from the list, simply consult the activities in the *Activities Book* on pages 78–120 to see which activities would be helpful.

Tying first lexicon words to communicative function

Owens (1996) provides further information about substantive and relational words, the two large semantic categories used to classify early single-word utterances.

Substantive words refer to specific entities that share perceptual or functional features. These are either agents (the source of the action) or objects (the recipient of the action).

Relational words refer to relations that the entity shares with itself or with other entities. These words make references across entities. The most frequent relational words are called *reflexive* because they relate to the object itself (Bloom & Lahey 1978). These reflexive words mark *existence*, (e.g., "this" to remark that this cookie is the one the child notices), *nonexistence* (e.g., "gone" when looking at an empty plate that the child expected would have a cookie on it), *disappearance* (e.g., "gone" when looking at the plate of cookies after the last one has been eaten), and *recurrence* (e.g., "more" to remark that Mom has put another cookie on the plate). Another type of relational words is called *action relational words* because they describe how objects relate through action or movement. These may include the *protoverbs* (e.g., *up, in, off*). There are three other types of relational words.

- *Location relational* words describe directional or spatial relationships between two objects (e.g., "shoe" when noticing the shoe falling off the dresser to the floor, "cat" when the cat is noted sleeping on the bed).

- *Possession relational* words show that an object is related to a person (e.g., "mine" when the child grabs his special blanket, "Daddy" when holding Dad's keys).

- *Attribution relational* words show the attributes, characteristics, or differences between objects (e.g., *big, ucky, dirty*).

Possession relational words and *attribution relational* words are considered state relations rather than location relations. They describe the state of the object (either an attribute of the object or who it belongs to).

It is important to tie the types of words (i.e., substantive or relational) to the way the child is using the word. The table in Appendix 9C (page 109) shows how relational words and substantive words are related to the communicative function served. It also gives examples of these words that might occur in the child's vocabulary at the one-word stage. Appendix 9D (page 110) provides a chart for tracking development of these communicative functions.

Semantic-Syntactic Relations

As two-word combinations emerge, children begin to express more advanced communicative/semantic functions by using the word order to convey meaning. Because word order rules and relationships are important in conveying the meaning, this is also the beginning of early syntax. It is not easy to separate form and meaning, and in fact, Lund and Duchan (1988) consider separating form and meaning an artificial distinction. Owens (1996) calls these early combination rules *semantic-syntactic*: "*Semantic* because the bases for combinations are meaning relations and *syntactic* because word order rules and relationships pertain." Initially word order may vary, but tends to stabilize before the child begins using grammatical markers, such as possessive.

The chart on the next page reflects Brown's (1973) description of these semantic-syntactic relations that can account for the majority of word combinations in toddlers' speech. These two-word combinations may be used to express a variety of communicative intents (pragmatic functions). This chart does not attempt to match the semantic-syntactic relation to all possible communicative intents, but some examples are provided. Appendix 9E (page 111) provides a chart for tracking development of semantic-syntactic relations.

Semantic-Syntactic Relation	Example	Notes	Possible Communicative Intent(s)

Modifier + head
   Attribute-entity
   Possessor-possession
 	
   Recurrence + X
	Bad dog
	Mama nose
	
	More juice
			Commenting on object
			Commenting on object; answering
			Requesting, commenting on object or action

Negative + x
   Nonexistence or
      Disappearance
 	
   Rejection
 	
   Denial
	No cookie
	All gone 'nana
	
	No bed
	
	Not shoe
		To indicate there is no cookie and that the banana has been eaten
		Note: This is the predominant type of negative used.
		To indicate child does not want to go to bed
		To indicate the item being held is not a shoe or to answer parent's *yes/no* question
			Commenting on object; requesting
			
			Protesting
			
			Commenting on object, answering

Demonstrative-entity	*That car*		Requesting, commenting on object, protesting
Entity-locative	*Bubby bed*	To indicate brother is in the bed	Commenting object
Action-locative	*Put in*	To indicate putting it in the box	Commenting on action, requesting, answering
Agent-action	*Bubby fall*		Commenting on action
Action-object	*Kiss baby*		Request, commenting on action
Agent-object	*Mama keys*	To indicate Mama is doing something to the keys	Commenting on action

Morphemes and Early Sentence Forms

As children move past the two-word stage, they begin to use morphemes and build other sentence types. These two aspects of expressive language (morphemes and sentence types) are discussed together, as it is difficult to discuss one without the other. Recall Brown's Stages of Language Development (1973) which indicate that morphological development occurs in Stage II and sentence form development begins in Stage III. (We will not attend to Stages IV and V because they usually occur after 36 months of age.)

Owens (1996) describes Brown's Stages of Language Development:

Stage	MLU	Approximate Age in Months	Characteristics
I	1.0-2.0	12-26	Linear semantic rules
II	2.0-2.5	27-30	Morphological development
III	2.5-3.0	31-34	Sentence-form development

Brown described fourteen morphemes whose development occurs across all five stages (not just the three stages seen in children under 36 months of age). Research by others (Bellugi & Brown 1964, Miller 1981) demonstrates that there is a wide range of when the use of these morphemes is mastered, but some children will begin to use all of them before the age of 36 months. These are listed in roughly the order in which they are mastered. Appendix 9F (page 112) provides a chart for tracking development of morphemes.

Morpheme	Example
Present progressive -*ing* (no auxiliary)	Dog barking
In	Dog in house
On	Dog on bed
Regular plural -*s*	Dogs
Irregular past tense	Broke
Possessive*s*	Dog's food all gone
Uncontractible copula (verb *to be* as main verb)	Dog is (in response to "Who is sick?")
Articles (e.g., *a*, *the*)	I want a dog.
Regular past tense -*ed*	The dog barked.
Regular third person -*s*	Dog barks
Irregular third person	does, has
Uncontractible auxiliary	Dog is (in response to "Who is barking?")
Contractible copula	Dog is sleepy. Dog's sleepy
Contractible auxiliary	Dog is eating. Dog's eating.

Owens (1996) also describes acquisition of sentence types. This information was based on approximately 50% of children using a structure. The approximate progression of this development is summarized on the next page.

Chapter 9: Intervention for Expressive Language

Declarative	Negative	Interrogative	Embedded	Conjoined
Agent + action *Dog bark*		Single words with rising inflection *Car? Eat?*		serial naming without *and* *shoes, socks*
Action + object *Kiss Mommy*		*What* and *where* questions *What that? Where juice?*		
Subject + verb + object *Me + get + ball*		That + X What + noun phrase + doing? Where + noun phrase + going? *That baby? What baby doing?* *Where Dad going?*	Prepositions *in* and *on, in bed, on foot*	*and*
Subject + copula + complement *Car + is + gone*	*no, not, don't can't*; negative is placed between subject and predicate *Car not going,* *Bobby can't reach*	What or where + subject + predicate; Inversion appears with copula in What/where + copula + subject *Where Sue put car?* *Where is Juan?*	*gonna, wanna, gotta*	
Subject + auxiliary + verb + object *Cat is licking me*				*but, so, or* and *if*
Subject + auxiliary + copula + X *Mommy will be home*	*won't*	Auxiliary verbs *do, can, have, be* and *will* in questions; inversion of subject and auxiliary verb in *yes/no* questions *Do you like it? Will you get it?*		

Adapted from Owens 1996

Appendix 9G (page 113) provides a form for tracking development of five main sentence types. For more in-depth analysis of syntax development, there are a variety of language sample analysis tools available. As you plan treatment, design activities to stimulate the use of specific morphemes and the use of these morphemes in early sentence types.

Tracking Development of Expressive Language

Because you will likely only see the child once a week, it is helpful if the caregivers keep track of new words and word combinations. If they keep such a journal, it can be an excellent starting place for your session. You can review any new words the child has used during the week. It is helpful if the caregiver records the situation(s) in which the word(s) were used, as this will give you some idea of the semantic and pragmatic function. You can provide an inexpensive notebook or use Appendix 9H (page 114) to help the caregiver organize her observations.

Intervention Techniques to Develop Expressive Language

Chapman and Terrell (1994) summarize some language intervention techniques to help develop specific word use.

Chapter 9: Intervention for Expressive Language

- *Focused stimulation* involves modeling many uses of the target language form. You have to structure the environment so that it is natural and also necessary to use the targeted word. For example, when pushing the child on a swing, the child might have to say "push" or "go" each time you let the swing stop. You can also say the word several times while the child is performing an action, and then ask, "What are you doing?" to prompt the child's use of the word. The prompt should appear as a natural part of the communication.

- Using scripts to specify the actors, actions, and props used to carry out the goals (Nelson 1986). *Scripts* are ordered sequences of actions. A script assumes that the child is familiar with the routine. A simple script for washing a baby doll is shown in the box. As each familiar step in the script is performed by the child, the general purpose word (e.g., *in* or *wash*) can be used and the child will know which event it is signaling. For example, if water has already been poured in the tub and you are holding the baby doll and say, "in," the child knows that "in" is signaling that it's time to put the doll in the tub. If the doll's body parts are always washed in the same order, then after the doll's face has been washed, your saying "wash" would signal to the child that the hands are next. You can prompt by touching the next body part while saying, "wash."

> Put the water *in* the tub
> Put the baby doll *in* the tub.
> Put the wash cloth *in* the tub.
> Put the soap *in* the tub.
> Put the soap *on* the washcloth.
> *Wash* the baby's face.
> *Wash* the baby's hands.
> *Wash* the baby's feet.
> *Wash* the baby's tummy.
> *Wash* the baby's back.
> *Wash* the baby's arms.
> *Wash* the baby.

- Give the child time to respond. Provide the stimulus (e.g., holding up the cookie) and wait to see if the child will give you the gesture or verbalization you desire.

- Withhold an expected object in a routine. If the child is engaged in a turn-taking game (e.g., rolling the ball back and forth), hold the ball. Wait to see if the child will use expressive language to indicate that he's ready for his turn.

- Forget to give the child something he needs. This works best for activities the child has completed on a routine basis. For example, perhaps you and the child have played "wash the baby doll" many times. You always get out the washtub, washcloth, baby doll, and shampoo. This time you get out the washtub, washcloth, and shampoo but purposely forget the baby doll.

- Make silly mistakes. This also works best with activities that are very routine for the child. For example, perhaps each day at lunchtime, the child's bowl and spoon are placed on the child's high chair tray, and then the food is poured into the bowl. To interrupt this routine, you might place the jar of food on the tray with a spoon but forget to open the jar. Wait to see if the child uses expressive language to request the missing action.

Setting Goals to Develop All Aspects of Expressive Language

The long-term goal for expressive language is that the child will exhibit optimal expressive language skills. However, short-term expressive goals are more complicated than those for other areas. In the other areas (e.g., receptive language), we used imitation as a method of prompting the child to help him develop a skill. In expressive language, imitation itself is a goal in early stages.

As mentioned at the beginning of the chapter, there are five aspects of expressive language that need to be addressed:

- communicative intent of the message (pragmatics)
- communicative function
- semantic-syntactic relations
- morphemes
- sentence types

Not all aspects are addressed with each goal. Communicative intent can be evidenced in any spontaneous gesture, vocalization, or utterance of any length. Communicative functions are reserved for describing single word utterances. Semantic-syntactic relations, morphemes, and sentence types describe word combinations.

- EG1 The child will increase imitation of vocalizations of non-speech sounds, speech sounds, and sound sequences.

  When a child is imitating vocalizations, he has no communicative (pragmatic) intent and of course there is no communicative function.

- EG2 The child will increase imitation of words.

  When the child is imitating words, he is working on development of specific communicative functions. You are probably also using these imitations in an activity with a specific outcome in mind (e.g., imitating the word *more* to request more juice), and are thus helping to develop communicative intent (pragmatics).

- EG3 The child will increase spontaneous use of vocalizations of non-speech sounds, speech sounds, and sound sequences.

  When the child begins to use these vocalizations (non-speech sounds, speech sounds, and sound sequences) spontaneously, there are no words so there is no communicative function. But the vocalizations may have a pragmatic intent (e.g., the child may be trying to protest or call attention).

EG4 and EG5 address the spontaneous use of words and combinations of words. It is important to view the development of spontaneous use of words and word combinations across the broad spectrum of skills you are trying to develop. If we limit ourselves to writing goals that simply state "The child will use more single words" or "The child will begin to use word combinations," then we are forgetting the breadth of functions of expressive language.

- EG4 The child will increase spontaneous use of single words.

    When a child begins to use single words, not only is he using the word to express a communicative intent (e.g., screaming "mine" to protest another child trying to take his cookie), but also using the words with a specific communicative function in mind (e.g., using the word *mine* to show possession).

- EG5 The child will increase spontaneous use of word combinations.

    When the child begins to use word combinations, we must continue to keep in mind not only the communicative intent of the message (pragmatics), but also the semantic-syntactic relations (if it is a two-word utterance) and the morphemes and sentence types for longer utterances.

The table below summarizes which aspects of language you are probably going to address related to each goal.

Goal	Communicative Intent	Communicative Function	Semantic-syntactic Relations	Morphemes	Sentence Structure
The child will increase imitation of vocalizations of non-speech sounds, speech sounds, and sound sequences. (EG1)					
The child will increase imitation of words. (EG2)	X	X			
The child will increase spontaneous use of vocalizations of non-speech sounds, speech sounds, and sound sequences. (EG3)	X				
The child will increase spontaneous use of single words. (EG4)	X	X			
The child will increase spontaneous use of word combinations. (EG5)	X		X	X	X

Making expressive goals even more complex are all the types of communicative intents, communicative functions, semantic-syntactic relations, and morphemes and sentence types the child needs to develop. Thus it is not enough to write a goal that the child will "develop the use of semantic-syntactic relations." You need to ensure you are stimulating development of a variety of different semantic-syntactic relations. You also need to remember that the child needs to develop those specific semantic-syntactic relations for different communicative (pragmatic) intents. The information provided earlier in the chapter about each of these aspects is summarized on the next page related to each of the five short-term expressive goals. The aspect(s) of language development you need to keep in mind when working on that goal and the different types (e.g., types of communicative intent) are also shown on the next page.

Chapter 9: Intervention for Expressive Language

Communicative Intent Types	Communicative Function Types	Semantic-syntactic Relations Types	Morpheme Types	Sentence Structure Types

Repeating/practicing
Calling attention
Requesting
  Object
  Action
  Information
Protesting
Commenting
  On object
  On action
Greeting
Answering
Acknowledging
	Negation
	  Nonexistence–
	    disappearance
	  Rejection
	  Denial
	Recurrence
	Existence
	Action on object
	Locative action
	Attribution
	Naming
	Possession
	Commenting
	Social Interaction
		Attribute-entity
		Possessor-possession
		Agent-action
		Action-object
		Agent-object
		Demonstrative-entity
		Entity-locative
		Action-locative
		Recurrence
		Nonexistence-
		  disappearance
		Rejection
		Denial
			Present progressive *-ing*
			In
			On
			Regular plural *-s*
			Irregular past tense
			Possessives
			Uncontractible copula
			Articles
			Regular past tense
			Regular third person
			Irregular third person
			Contractible copula
			Contractible auxiliary
				Declarative
				Negative
				Interrogative
				Embedded
				Conjoined

The activities for this chapter (pages 78–120 in the *Activities Book*) include the goals listed on pages 99 and 100. The specific communicative intents, communicative functions, semantic-syntactic relations, morphemes, and/or sentence types are included in the activities. With slight modifications, you can easily address other intents, functions, relations, or morphemes.

Some activities have tips about additional words/word combinations that could be stimulated. This was done to provide many activities that relate to the development of a core lexicon. (See Appendix 9B, pages 107–108.) However, because those are not the objectives of that particular activity, they have been added to the activity description in the *Activities Book* in italics. The intents, functions, relations, morphemes, and/or sentence types are also marked in italics. (See Activity E20b and E26a on the next page for an example.)

> A special note regarding the two imitation goals in this chapter:
>
> - EG1 The child will increase imitation of vocalizations of non-speech sounds, speech sounds, and sound sequences.
>
> - EG2 The child will increase imitation of words.
>
> These goals were matched to treatment objectives when the actual objective is imitation (e.g., Activity E27 echoes prominent or last word spoken) or if imitation is inherent in the treatment objective (e.g., child will vocalize in response to singing). In this example, the child is not expected to initiate the vocalization, so it seems inherently imitative in nature. Most treatment objectives intend for the child to produce the utterance, word, or phrase spontaneously. Therefore, even though imitation is used during the related activity, the applicable spontaneous goal is selected and the communicative intent(s), communicative function(s), semantic-syntactic relations, morphemes, and/or sentence types were selected to describe how the goal is used in that activity if the child were doing it spontaneously.

Chapter 9: Intervention for Expressive Language

E20b

Treatment Objective: The child will use early-developing modifiers.

Goal: The child will increase spontaneous use of single words. (EG4)

Communicative Intent (pragmatics)	Communicative Function
Commenting	Attribution
On object	Negation
Requesting	*Non-existence or disappearance*
Action	*Action on object*

Activity: Icky   **Expected age:** 12–15 months

Materials/Toys: construction paper, brightly colored small pieces of paper to glue on the construction paper, glue stick

Have the child sit at a small table or in his high chair with the tray in place. Put some glue on the back of one of the small pieces of paper and then stick it on the construction paper. Encourage the child to watch. Wait and see if the child asks for a turn. *Stimulate the use of "Do" (e.g., "You wanna do it?" or "Wanna?")*. Then put lots of glue on another small piece of paper, hand it to the child, and say, "Your turn. Stick it on." The child will inevitably get glue on himself. When he does, say, "Icky! It feels icky." If necessary, gently take the child's finger and touch some glue. **Prompt** by saying, "Ick." When you put the glue away, stimulate use of *"All gone"* or *"All done."*

Note: Children with sensory deficits may find this activity upsetting because they may not like the feel of the glue. If you note such sensory issues, an occupational therapy consult may be indicated.

This is *requesting an action* (communicative intent). The communicative function is *action on object*, so those two are italicized.

Using the words "all gone" or "all done" achieves the same intent (commenting on an object) as the main word you are stimulating ("ick"). Therefore, the words "commenting on object" are not italicized. The function is different, however, so *negation/non-existence* is italicized. (The function for "ick" is attribution.)

Activity E26a stimulates the use of the word "more." If the child uses "more," the communicative intent is **requesting an object** (e.g., "more bubbles") and the communicative function is **recurrence**. The activity also states: *"If the child wants a turn blowing, this is a good opportunity to stimulate 'Gimme bubbles,' 'Wanna blow?,' or 'me.' "* Those additional targets address *requesting an action* as the communicative intent and *action on object* as the communicative function, and are also marked in italics.

E26a

Treatment Objective: The child will ask for "more."

Goal: The child will increase spontaneous use of single words. (EG4)

Communicative Intent (pragmatics)	Communicative Function
Requesting	Recurrence
Object	*Action on object*
Action	

Activity: Bubble Blowing   **Expected age:** 15–18 months

Materials/Toys: bubbles

Sit on the floor with the child facing you. Blow one set of bubbles. Then say "Let's blow some more." Blow more bubbles and say, "More. See? More bubbles. Let's blow some more." Before blowing more bubbles, ask the child, "What do you want?" The expected response is "more." If the child fails to say *"more,"* **prompt** with "Tell me what you want" or "I think we need *more* bubbles. Tell me 'more.' "

If the child wants a turn blowing, this is a good opportunity to stimulate "Gimme bubbles," "Wanna blow?," or "me." You can also hand the bubbles to the child with the lid on tight to stimulate the use of the word "help."

Note: This activity can be used to combine speech and sign by saying the word *more* and demonstrating the sign for *more* at the same time. A picture exchange system could also be used with the child handing a picture of bubbles to the clinician.

Italics indicate that you could address these additional language targets.

Italics indicate that these are related to additional language; not the main purpose of the activity.

Chapter 9: Intervention for Expressive Language

Sometimes the objective of an activity addresses more than one communicative intent, function, semantic-syntactic relation, morpheme, and/or sentence type. In that case, you will find more than one listed. It should be clear from the activity which one is being developed by which part of the activity.

Activity E28 has the child naming objects. If the child names the object spontaneously when you pull it out of the bag, the communicative intent is *commenting on an object*. If, however, you have to ask the child what it is and he responds, the intent is *answering*. Thus, both of those types of communicative intents are listed. If the activity is modified (as is often the case when following the child's lead), remember that all possibilities are not listed. Use your judgment to determine what you have addressed. For example, if the child doesn't like doing this activity and starts saying "No," then you have addressed "protesting" as an intent.

Some activities are so open-ended that any of the communicative intent(s), communicative function(s), semantic-syntactic relations, morphemes, and/or sentence types might be targeted. If that is the case, the area heading remains listed but not the specific targets. The treatment objective in Activity E41 is "sings phrases of songs." Depending on the song selected, any of the communicative intent(s), communicative function(s), semantic-syntactic relations, morphemes, and/or sentence types might be demonstrated by the words in the song.

The activities in the *Activities Book* on pages 78–120 should help address the goals listed on pages 99–100. The activities correspond to the treatment objectives listed in the chart on pages 104–105 (also listed in the *Activities Book* on pages 76–77).

Expressive Ages of Acquisition/Treatment Objectives

Expected age of development	Short-term goal (EG)	Treatment Objectives	Activities to help achieve treatment objectives*
3–6 months	1	Vocalizes in response to singing	E1
	1	Takes turns vocalizing	E2 a, b
	3	Produces "raspberries"	E3
	3	Stops babbling when another person vocalizes	E4
6–9 months	3	Vocalizes four different syllables	E5
	1	Vocalizes two-syllable combination	E6
	3	Vocalizes in response to objects that move	E7 a, b, c
	1	Imitates duplicated syllables	E8 a, b
9–12 months	4	Says "Mama" or "Dada" meaningfully	E9 a, b
	1	Imitates consonant and vowel combinations	E10 a, b, c, d
	1	Imitates non-speech sounds	E11 a, b, c
	1	Imitates correct number of syllables/sounds heard	E12 a, b
	4	Says one or two words spontaneously	E13
	2	Imitates names of familiar objects	E14 a, b
12–15 months	3	Varies pitch when vocalizing	E15 a, b
	2	Tries to sing with familiar song	E16
	2	Imitates new words	E17 a, b
	4	Uses exclamatory expressions (e.g., "Uh-oh," "No-no")	E18
	1	Imitates three animal sounds	E19
	4	Uses early-developing modifiers	E20 a, b, c
15–18 months	4	Answers questions with one word	E21
	4	Uses word to call attention to something	E22
	4	Uses word to comment on action or object	E23
	4	Uses word to request action	E24
	5	Asks, "What's that?"	E25
	4	Asks for "more"	E26 a, b
	2	Echoes prominent or last word spoken	E27
	4	Names five to seven familiar objects on request	E28
18–21 months	5	Uses attribute-entity	E29
	5	Uses possessor-possession	E30
	5	Uses agent-action	E31
	5	Uses action-object	E32
	5	Uses agent-object	E33
	4	Uses vocalizations and gestures to request toys or food	E34
	4, 5	Names a few pictures	E35
21–24 months	5	Uses entity-locative	E36
	5	Uses action-locative	E37
	4	Uses own name to refer to self	E38 a, b
	4, 5	Uses early pronouns occasionally	E39

*See pages 78–120 in the *Activities Book*.

Chapter 9: Intervention for Expressive Language

Expected age of development	Short-term goal (EG)	Treatment Objectives	Activities to help achieve treatment objectives*
24–27 months	2	Imitates two numbers or unrelated words on request	E40 a, b
	5	Sings phrases of songs	E41
	4, 5	Names objects in photographs	E42
	4, 5	Uses action words	E43
27–30 months	4, 5	Names one color	E44
	4, 5	Consistently refers to self by pronouns	E45
	5	Uses two sentence types	E46
	4	Responds to greetings consistently	E47
	5	Uses past tense	E48
	5	Requests actions or objects	E49
	4, 5	Names five pictures	E50
	5	Uses negation	E51
30–33 months	4	Answers questions with "yes" or "no"	E52
	2	Imitates series of three numbers or unrelated words	E53
	4, 5	Uses plurals	E54
	5	Uses prepositions	E55
	4, 5	States gender	E56
	4	States first and last name	E57
33–36 months	5	Uses verb forms	E58
	5	Asks "what," "who," and "where" questions	E59 a, b, c
	4	Counts to three	E60 a, b, c, d
	5	Recites a few nursery rhymes	E61

*See pages 78–120 in the *Activities Book*.

Tracking Development of Communicative Intent (Pragmatics)

Child's name _____ Person interacting with child _____

Write the date observed and the utterance in the appropriate box.

Answer	Acknowledge	Seek/Call Attention	Comment on Action	Comment on Object	Request Objects

Request Actions	Protest	Greeting	Practice/Repeating	Request Information

Adapted from Dore 1975 and Owens 1996

Appendix 9A

Relating Core Lexicon to Treatment Objectives

Appendix 9B

Vocabulary Word to Be Developed	Activities that Address that Word*
all done	E17a, E32
all gone	E17a, E34
angry word (e.g., *poo*, *ick*, *No!*)	E20a, E20b
ball	E12a, E14b, E28, E49
big	E17a, E29, E54
block	E14a, E18, E28, E45
blow	E20a, E26a, E31, E40a, E46, E54
boo	E6
bye-bye	E47a, E47b
car	E14a, E28, E29
(child's own name)	E38a, E38b, E57
close	E23
come	E17b, E37
cry	E26, E31, E40a, E46, E48, E58
dance	E31, E40a, E46, E48, E58
do	E20b
down	E15b, E17b
drink	E21, E31
drop	E29, E30, E58
eat	E21, E26b, E27
fall	E31, E40a, E46
(favorite activity/toy)	E17a, E44
(favorite food)	E34
get	E29
get down	E21
gimme	E26a, E39, E49
give	E3a, E45, E49
go	E8a, E17b, E24, E37
help	E24, E26a
here	E18, E52
Hi	E9a, E9b, E47
hug	E40a, E46, E48, E58
in	E28, E36, E37, E52, E55
inside	E23, E36

*See pages 78–120 in the *Activities Book*.

continued on next page

Relating Core Lexicon to Treatment Objectives | Appendix 9B

Vocabulary Word to Be Developed	Activities that Address that Word*
jump	E31, E40a, E46, E48, E58
kick	E3a, E32, E58
kiss	E29, E31, E32, E46
(least favorite food)	E21
make	E39
me	E26a, E33b, E39, E45, E49
more	E26a, E26b, E34
my/mine	E30, E38a, E55
(names of significant others)	E8b, E9a, E9b, E38
night-night	E12b
no	E10b, E51, E52, E54
off	E17b, E30, E36, E37, E55
on	E18, E30, E36, E39, E41, E55
open	E23
out	E17a, E17b, E23, E36, E37
pull	E25
push	E29, E43
read	E35, E46
ride	E29, E31, E46
run	E31, E40a, E46
see	E17a, E22, E32
shake	E17a, E20a, E21, E30
sit	E31, E40a, E46
stand	E31, E40a, E46
stop	E17b, E58
tear	E31
that	E22, E39, E44
there	E17a, E39
throw	E21, E30, E32
up	E15b, E17b, E37
walk	E31, E40a, E46, E48, E58
wanna	E20b, E26a, E27
wash	E21, E31
you	E38b, E40a
your	E30, E38a

*See pages 78–120 in the *Activities Book*.

Appendix 9C

Development of Communicative Functions

Substantive and Relational Categories	Semantic Class Distinctions		Communicative Function to Be Served
	Substantive	**Relational**	
Agent or object	*Mama, Dada, shoe, cup, dog, car,* etc. when looking at the object and naming it to acknowledge it is there		Naming
	Mama, Dada, dog when commenting that the person or object is doing something (comment on action) or when an object is being acted upon (says *ball* when it is rolling)		Commenting
One word reflexive relational		/////////////	Negation
		all gone, all done, away, gone, or name of object with rising inflection (*shoe?*)	Nonexistence or disappearance
		No (when child is told to stop doing something)	Rejection
		No (when Mom holds up bottle and asks "Do you want this?")	Denial
		more, again, nuther	Recurrence
		this, that, there, here, whazzat? (while pointing)	Existence
Action relational		*get, do, make, throw, tear, kiss, wash*	Action on Object
Location relational		*up, down, out, door* (when door is opening)	Locative Action
Possession relational		*Mama, Dada, shoe, cup, dog,* etc. when indicating the person or object belongs to the child. May also use the word *mine*. Could also point to an object and say "Mama" to indicate that object belongs to Mama	Possession
Attribution relational		*icky, hot, pretty, uh oh* (indicates a mismatch with child's expectations of the attribute)	Attribution

Adapted from Owens 1996, Lahey & Bloom 1977, Lahey 1988, McCune-Nicolich 1981, and Paul 1995

Appendix 9D

Tracking Development of Communicative Functions

Child's name _____

Write in the words and dates used.

Substantive and Relational Categories	Semantic Class Distinctions		Communicative Function to Be Served
	Substantive	**Relational**	
Agent or object			Naming
			Commenting
One word reflexive relational			Negation
			Nonexistence or Disappearance
			Rejection
			Denial
			Recurrence
			Existence
Action relational			Action on Object
Location relational			Locative Action
Possession relational			Possession
Attribution relational			Attribution

Adapted from Owens 1996, Lahey & Bloom 1977, Lahey 1988, McCune-Nicolich 1981, and Paul 1995

Therapy Guide
The Early Intervention Kit

Copyright © 2004 LinguiSystems, Inc.

Tracking Semantic-Syntactic Relations

Child's name _____   Person interacting with child _____

Write in the semantic-syntactic relation and date observed.

Semantic-Syntactic Relation	Examples	Date:	Date:	Date:	Date:	Date:
Modifier + X Attribute-entity Possessor-possession Recurrence	*bad dog* *Mama nose* *more juice*					
Negative + X Nonexistence or disappearance Rejection Denial	*no cookie, all gone* *'nana* *no bed* *not shoe*					
Demonstrative-entity	*that car*					
Entity-locative	*Bobby bed*					
Action-locative	*put in*					
Agent-action	*Bobby fall*					
Action-object	*kiss baby*					
Agent-object	*Mama keys*					

Appendix 9E

Adapted from Owens 1996, Bloom 1973, Brown 1973, and Schlesinger 1971

Therapy Guide
The Early Intervention Kit

Copyright © 2004 LinguiSystems, Inc.

Appendix 9F

Tracking Development of Morphemes

Child's name _____ Person interacting with child _____

Write in examples of morphemes used and dates heard.

Present Progressive -ing (no auxiliary)	In	On	Regular Plural -s	Irregular Past Tense	Possessives	Uncontractable Copula (verb *to be* as main verb)

Articles	Regular Past Tense -ed	Regular Third Person -s	Irregular Third Person	Uncontractible Auxiliary	Contractible Copula	Contractible Auxiliary

Adapted from McLean & Snyder-McLean 1978, Bellugi & Brown 1964, Brown 1973, and Miller 1981

Therapy Guide
The Early Intervention Kit Copyright © 2004 LinguiSystems, Inc.

Tracking Development of Basic Sentence Types

Child's name _____

Person interacting with child _____

Write in the child's utterance and the date heard. Then place a checkmark to indicate the sentence type.

Date	Utterance	Declarative	Negative	Interrogative	Embedded	Conjoined

Adapted from Owens 1996

Appendix 9G

New Words

Child's name _____

Use this form to keep track of your child's expressive language development.

Word or Word Combinations	When Word/words Used	Did the child say the word on his/her own or imitate you?	Who was child speaking to?	Date

Appendix 9H

Adapted from Owens 1996

Chapter 10

Intervention for Sound Production Development

The development of sound production abilities begins long before meaningful sound production. The speech-like and non-speech-like sounds that infants produce during the first year of life are precursors to future sound development and communication. The vocalizations are also tied very closely to the child's motor development. If the child has impairments in motor development, the child may have impaired ability to vocalize. For example, the child with low muscle tone may have decreased breath support. Her vocalizations may be shorter and sound different from a child who has no problems with muscle tone. The chart below reflects the different levels of motor skill and how they relate to early sound production.

Level(s) of Motor Skill	Brief Description of Communicative Skill Obtained	Anticipated Age of Onset
1. Reflexive	Sustained crying Fasting sounds (e.g., contented sound made, not during feeding) Vegetative sounds Quasi-resonant nucleus (i.e., small grunt) Fully resonant nucleus (i.e., a sound produced with an open mouth that is harsh, not vowel-like)	0–2 months
2. Control of phonation	Single vowel Combination of vowel with trill, friction consonant, or nasal murmur Syllabic nasal consonant (e.g., /m/) Chuckle Sustained laughter	2–4 months
Expansion 3. Control of articulation 4. Control of pitch	Prolonged inspiratory sounds Squeal Series of vowels Vowels with glide Isolated prolonged consonant Series of isolated consonants Marginal babbling	5–6 months
5. Babbling: syllable production	Consonant-vowel (CV) syllable Reduplicated (repeated) CV syllable series Simple, non-reduplicated CV syllable series Yell	7–9 months
6. New syllable types 7. Expressive jargon	Vowels /i/ as in *see* and /u/ as in *too* Other rounded vowels (e.g., /o/ as in *toe*) Diphthongs (e.g., /au/ as in *out*) Syllables other than CV Whisper More complex non-reduplicated syllable series Jargon	10–18 months

Stark et al. (1988) originally hypothesized seven levels of vowel development. In the schema, they have combined some of the levels.
Reprinted with permission from J. Blackman (Ed.), (1995), *Treatment options in early intervention*. Gaithersburg, MD: Aspen Publishers, Inc.

Chapter 10: Intervention for Sound Production Development

From six months to one year of age, the child's vocalizations will include several forms of babbling. By the ninth or tenth month, the child's babbling becomes smoother and more regular in rhythm and begins to include some consonant-vowel combinations. Around 12 months of age, the child begins to use *jargoning*. Jargoning builds on the consonant-vowel combinations by adding a variety of intonation patterns and inflections. These may sound similar to adult conversational speech (Linder 1990).

Another way to look at sound development and levels of vocalization is according to the communicative context or intent with which they are produced. This is reflected in the chart below.

Level	Brief Description of Context	Anticipated Age of Onset
	Sounds according to context	
1. Reflexive	Cry Discomfort Small grunts Vegetative	0–2 months

2. Reactive	Comfort
	   In response to persons
	   In response to objects
	Neutral
	   In response to persons
	   In response to objects
	Chuckle
	Laughter
		2–4 months

3. Activity	Visual attention to objects Objects in mouth Manipulation of objects (e.g., banging, shaking) Locomotion Other movement	4–6 months
	Sounds according to intent	
1. Personal	Self-conscious expressions of feeling Showing off	7–9 months
2. Instrumental/ regulatory	Requesting object Requesting activity Rejecting object Rejecting activity	9–12 months
3. Interactional	Greetings Ritual exchanges Imitation of adult Commenting on objects Commenting on activity Noticing object	12–15 months
4. Heuristic/imaginative and other	Onomatopoeic sounds (e.g., animal and car noises) Agreement ("Yes") Disagreement ("No") Naming Requesting names Imaginative play Commenting on appearance/disappearance of objects	16–24 months

Adapted with permission from Stark, R. (1995). Early language intervention: When, why, how? In J. A. Blackman (Ed.), *Treatment Options in Early Intervention* (pp. 25-36). Gaithersburg, MD: Aspen Publishers, Inc.

Information is available about the ages of expected development of production of certain consonants and vowels and is shown in the chart below and on page 118.

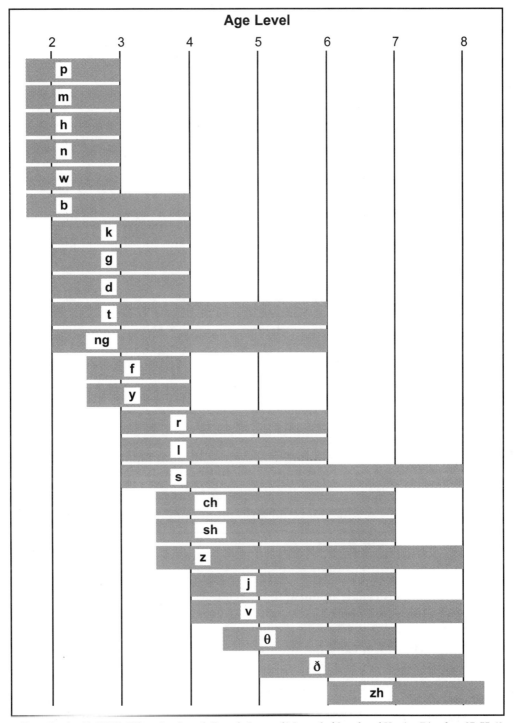

From Sander, E. (1972). When Are Speech Sounds Learned? *Journal of Speech and Hearing Disorders, 37*, 55-63
Used by permission.

The gray bar corresponding to each sound starts at the median age of customary articulation. It stops at an age level at which 90% of all children are customarily producing the sound.

Chapter 10: Intervention for Sound Production Development

Age level at which 75 percent or more subjects correctly produced given phoneme from *Photo Articulation Test* (PAT, Pendergast et al. 1969)

	Articulation Behaviors			
24 months	t- n- -n k- g- p- -p b-	m- -m h- aʊ u æ ɔ ə aɪ	ɛ ɑ i e ʌ ʊ o ɪ ɔɪ	
28 months	-s d- -d	-k f- -f	-ŋ j-	
32 months	-t -r	-b w-	ɝ	
36 months	s- -l	-g	ɚ	
40 months	-ʃ l-	bl- r- br-	tr- -v	
44 months	ʃ- tʃ-	-tʃ fl-		
48 months	sp- st-	kl- ð-	-ð -ʒ	
48+ months	z- -z	θ- -θ	v- ju	-dʒ dʒ-

Material from the SICD-R, Copyright © 1975, 1984 by Don Lea Hedrick, Elizabeth M. Prather and Annette R. Tobin, Copyright © 2002 by Western Psychological Services. Reprinted with permission of the publisher, Western Psychological Services, 12031 Wilshire Boulevard, Los Angeles, California, 90025, U.S.A. Not to be reprinted in whole or in part for any additional purpose without the expressed, written permission of the publisher. All rights reserved.

Analysis of this and other data reveal that many two-year-olds are able to produce many phonemes correctly in most positions of the word. However, the number of phonemes produced correctly in the initial position is always greater than the number produced in the final position (Stoel-Gammon 1985, 1989). Stoel-Gammon (1994) also points out that the inventory of speech sounds and syllable and word shapes the child is able to produce expands considerably between the ages of 24 and 36 months. She cites two studies (Sander 1972, Prather et al. 1975) that showed that by the age of three, at least half of children demonstrated customary production of 16 to 20 consonant phonemes of English (of the total 24). At 24 months of age, overall vowel accuracy exceeds 75%, with some vowels above 90% (Hare 1983).

If the child is having trouble producing a particular consonant, the following tips for manually eliciting early-developing sounds may help the child achieve accurate production. (Note: Wear latex gloves for any oral-motor manipulation in or near the child's mouth. Check the child's medical records for any latex allergy.)

Chapter 10: Intervention for Sound Production Development

Sound (Phoneme)	Manual Cues to Stimulate Sound Production	Touch Cues to Stimulate Sound Production
/m/	Manually squeeze the child's lips during humming or oral voicing.	
/b/	While the child is humming, manually pull her lips open.	Touch your index finger to your lips and then pull it away quickly as you say the sound.
/p/	Manually open and close the child's lips during blowing.	Same as /b/.
/n/	Alternately lift and then lower the child's tongue tip with a tongue blade while the child is humming or voicing orally. Also, have the child imitate tongue clicking.	Touch your finger to the child's nose.
/d/	Alternately lift and then lower the child's tongue tip with a tongue blade while the child is humming or voicing orally. Also, have the child imitate tongue clicking.	Tap the child's upper lip with your index finger as the sound is made.
/l/	Alternately lift and then lower the child's tongue tip with a tongue blade while the child is humming or voicing orally. Also, have the child imitate tongue clicking.	Place the tip of your index finger and the tip of your middle finger at the corners of the child's top lip to hold the lips in a retracted position. This will eliminate the common substitution of /w/. Then show the child how to lift her tongue to make the /l/.
/t/	Alternately lift and lower the child's tongue tip with a tongue blade while the child is producing /h/ or blowing air.	Tap the child's upper lip with your index finger as the sound is made.
/k/	During exhalation of air, push the tongue posteriorly with a tongue blade until the dorsum makes contact with the soft palate. Then release the pressure of the tongue blade to lower the tongue immediately. You can also have the child lie on her back to help her tongue fall posteriorly into the oral cavity.	Tap under the child's chin with your index finger.
/g/	While the child is producing any vowel, push the tongue posteriorly with a tongue blade until the dorsum makes contact with the soft palate, then lower the tongue immediately.	Same as /k/.
/f/	During exhalation of air or during blowing, push the child's lower lip so it touches her upper teeth.	
/s/	Have the child produce /t/ 8–10 times in a row very quickly and hold the last /t/ produced.	"Draw" a line up the child's arm from her hand to her shoulder using your index finger as the sound is produced, or draw a horizontal line with your index finger under the child's lower lip.
/sh/	If the child can produce /s/, gently squeeze her lips into a rounded position and have her produce the sound.	Gently squeeze her lips into a rounded position and have her produce the sound.

continued on next page

Therapy Guide
The Early Intervention Kit

Chapter 10: Intervention for Sound Production Development

Sound (Phoneme)	Manual Cues to Stimulate Sound Production	Touch Cues to Stimulate Sound Production
/j/	Introduce with the vowel /ɪ/ or /i/ and move to another vowel according to the word desired (e.g., /i→æ/ = "yeah," /ɪ→ɛ+l/ = "yell").	
/w/	Introduce with the vowel /u/ and move to another vowel according to the word desired (e.g., /u→a/, /u→ʌ/).	Use your fingers to help mold the child's mouth into the rounded position for /u/.

The development of many early vowel sounds relies on the child listening to your production and then imitating. (Activities for sound production are provided in the *Activities Book*, pages 124–150). There are some vowels that can be simulated with manual manipulation of the lips. They may not sound exact because the child may not have her tongue in the correct position. Ask the child to try to approximate the vowel sound you model. Use the following tips to refine the sound.

/u/   When the child is vocalizing, use your fingers to round her lips.

/i/   When the child is vocalizing, use your fingers to pull her lips into a smile.

/au/   When the child is vocalizing, pull her jaw into an open position.

Adapted from Blakely, R. (1983). Treatment of developmental apraxia of speech. In W. H. Perkins (Ed.), *Dysarthria and apraxia*. NY: Thieme-Stratton, Inc. and Bashir, A., Grahamjones, F., & Bostwick, R. (1984). "A touch-cue method of therapy for developmental verbal apraxia." *Seminars in Speech and Language, 5,* (2).

Young children may not produce the phoneme accurately when they are first learning it. That is, there may be some distortion. Some errors are considered developmental. For example, if a slight frontal lisp on production of /s/ is seen in a young child, you should model the accurate production and try to get the child to achieve accurate production. Some errors are not developmental (e.g., a lateral lisp) so you might take a more aggressive approach to eliminate the error.

In addition to helping the child develop the ability to produce different phonemes according to expected ages of production, you must also be aware of how the child's phonology is developing. Phonology is the rule-based sound system of language. By the time a child has approximately 25 words, she is already demonstrating an emerging phonological system. This means she has an understanding of how sounds in her environment are combined (Hodson & Paden 1983).

Children who demonstrate phonological errors often have highly unintelligible speech. Assessment using one of the phonological tools described in Chapter 5 (Appendix 5A, pages 61–64) is appropriate in order to plan a phonological approach to improve the child's intelligibility. For children who have phonological disorders, the goal is to establish the use of appropriate phonological patterns to replace the abnormal phonological processes. For example, final consonant deletion is an abnormal phonological process. Using consonants at the end of syllables is the appropriate phonological pattern you would want to develop.

Most information about phonological development has been gleaned from research with children over a wide age range, not just in children under the age of three. However, in the study by Dyson and Paden in 1983, the subjects were 23 to 35 months old at the beginning of data collection. The authors found that only the abnormal processes of gliding of liquids and cluster reduction were frequent. Therefore, it is clear that children nearing the age of three should be largely intelligible. However, abnormal phonological processes are still present in two-year-olds as indicated by other things we know about the phonological development of two-year-olds.

- Clusters are just emerging.
- Fricatives and affricates are not used.
- Stridency is often deleted.

The chart shows a summary of basic phonological processes that disappear by age three. Those phonological processes that continue past age 3-0 are not included. The age listed is the age at which the process (which is abnormal) should disappear and be replaced by a normal pattern. For example, the phonological process of fronting should disappear between age two and a half to three and should be replaced by the pattern of using back sounds.

Phonological Process	Age to Disappear
Prevocalic consonant deletion	2-0
Postvocalic consonant deletion	2-4
Prevocalic voicing of consonants	2-4
Weak syllable deletion	2-5 to 3-0
Fronting of /k, g/	2-6 to 3-0
Consonant harmony	2-6 to 3-0
Dimunitization	2-6
Final consonant deletion	3-0
Reduplication	3-0
Prevocalic voicing	3-0
Stopping of fricatives and affricates	3-0

Adapted from Grunwell, P. (1987). *Clinical phonology*. (2nd ed.) Baltimore: Williams & Wilkins; Khan, L. & Lewis, N. (1986). *Khan-Lewis phonological analysis*. Circle Pines, MN: American Guidance Service; and Stoel-Gammon, C. & Dunn, D. (1985). *Normal and disordered phonology in children*. Baltimore: University Park Press.

Therefore, before the age of two, you probably would not address any phonological process, but between the ages of two and three, you might begin to try to develop some specific phonological patterns such as:

- consistent use of consonants at the beginning of syllables
- consistent use of consonants at the end of syllables
- ability to use a voiceless consonant at the beginning of a syllable
  (e.g., in CV words like *pie, two, key*)
- eliminating the added "ee" at the end of words (e.g., *horsie, doggie*)

For more information on how to use a phonological approach to therapy, several books are listed in the reference list on pages 172–183 (e.g., Hodson & Paden 1983, Bernthal & Bankson 1981). When addressing sound production or phonological pattern development goals, they should be coordinated with appropriate expressive language goals. For example, if you are addressing development of the consonant /d/, and the child is also working on using more single words, you might use the words *down, dog, dig, dad*, and *don't* for language development. If working on a phonological goal to increase use of final consonants, and the target phoneme is final /p/, the language activities might include the action words *up* and *jump*.

Chapter 10: Intervention for Sound Production Development

The activities in the *Activities Book* on pages 124–150 should help address the following goals. The activities correspond to the treatment objectives listed in the chart on pages 123–124 (also listed in the *Activities Book* on pages 122–123).

Goals, Treatment Objectives, and Activities for Sound Production Development

Long-term goal
  The child will speak intelligibly as compared to developmental age peers.

Short-term goals

  SG1 The child will imitate target consonants in isolation.

  SG2 The child will imitate target consonants in words.

  SG3 The child will produce target consonants in words.

  SG4 The child will imitate target vowels in isolation.

  SG5 The child will imitate target vowels in words.

  SG6 The child will produce target vowels in words.

  SG7 The child will produce target consonants in connected speech.

  SG8 The child will produce target vowels in connected speech.

  SG9 The child will demonstrate mastery of phonological patterns.

There are nine goals for sound production, ranging from imitation of the sound in isolation to use of the sounds in connected speech. As written, most activities are geared toward imitation or production at the word level (and hence, those goals are referenced on each treatment activity: Goals 2 and 3 for consonants and Goals 5 and 6 for vowels).

Any of these activities could be adapted for production of the sound in isolation by modeling a sound from the target word (e.g., modeling just the /p/ instead of the word *pop*). Therefore, the goal for isolation consonants (Goal 1), is indicated in parenthesis in the chart on the next page, but won't be listed on the actual activity. However, the goal for isolation vowels (Goal 4) is referenced on each appropriate treatment activity.

In addition, any of these activities (vowels or consonants) could be adapted for producing the target in connected speech by increasing the length of utterance in which the target word is modeled and then expected. Therefore, Goals 7 and 8 are also indicated in parenthesis, and won't appear on the actual treatment activity. The phonologically-focused activities have only Goal 9 listed. There are no specific activities written for these, but rather a reference given to other activities that can be used to stimulate use of that pattern.

Therapy Guide
The Early Intervention Kit

Chapter 10: Intervention for Sound Production Development

Sound Production Ages of Acquisition/Treatment Objectives

Expected age of development	Short-term goal (SG)	Treatment Objectives	Activities to help achieve treatment objectives*
24–27 months	(1), 2, 3, (7)	Uses these consonants in the indicated position of words: Initial /t/ Initial /n/ Initial /k/ Initial /g/ Initial /p/ Initial /m/ Initial /h/ Final /n/ Final /p/ Final /m/	S1a, b S2a, b S3a, b S4a, b S5a, b S6a, b S7a, b S8a, b S9a, b S10a, b
	4, 5, 6, (8)	Produces these vowels: ɔ u æ ɑɪ ɛ ɪ e oʊ (o) i ɔɪ	S11a, b S12a, b S13a, b S14a, b S15a, b S16a, b S17a, b S18a, b S19a, b S20a, b
	9	Consistently uses prevocalic consonants	S21
27–30 months	(1), 2, 3, (7)	Uses these consonants in the indicated position of words: Initial /d/ Initial /f/ Initial /dʒ/ Final /s/ Final /d/ Final /k/ Final /f/ Final /ŋ/	S22a, b, c, d S23a, b, c S24a, b, c, d S25a, b S26a, b S27a, b S28a, b S29a, b
	9	Produces consonants in final position of VC or CVC words	S30
	9	Consistently uses voiceless consonants in the prevocalic position	S31
	9	Stops using diminutives	S32

*See pages 124–150 in the *Activities Book*.

Therapy Guide
The Early Intervention Kit

Chapter 10: Intervention for Sound Production Development

Expected age of development	Short-term goal (SG)	Treatment Objectives	Activities to help achieve treatment objectives*
30–33 months	(1), 2, 3, (7)	Uses these consonants in the indicated position of words: Initial /w/ Final /t/ Final /r/ Final /b/	S33a, b S34a, b, c S35a, b, c S36a, b, c
33–36 months	(1), 2, 3, (7)	Uses these consonants in the indicated position of words: Initial /s/ Final /l/ Final /g/	S37a, b S38a, b S39a, b
	9	Includes even weak syllables when using multisyllabic words	S40

*See pages 124–150 in the *Activities Book*.

Chapter 11

Augmentative and Alternative Communication

by Jennifer Perry Blevins

Augmentative and alternative communication (AAC) is an important component of intervention for children under three years of age. Special knowledge and skills are needed to provide services in this area so this chapter is not meant to be all-inclusive. Rather the goal of this chapter is to provide basic suggestions for implementing the use of AAC with this young population. In the case of the birth-to-three population, the focus of AAC is on supplementing (augmenting) and replacing (finding alternatives for) spoken words to improve a child's communication. This chapter focuses on low technology interventions to improve communication as these are most often used with very young children. Other helpful resources are listed in Appendix 11A (pages 135–136) to provide more information about AAC.

Communication is essential at all ages. Initially, communication may be an infant's cry to signal a need to be fed. As children grow and their language develops, they typically use spoken words and then later, written language to communicate. However, for some children, these skills may be delayed or may never be acquired. In either case, these individuals may benefit from an AAC system. AAC is the supplementation or replacement of natural speech and/or writing (Lloyd et al. 1997). AAC systems may include gestures, signs, communication boards, line drawings, words and/or the alphabet, books of photographs, and computer-based voice output communication aids (Light & Binger 1998).

While many view AAC-based communication as the solution of last resort (Ballinger 1999), many studies have shown that the introduction of AAC frequently has a positive effect on speech in that speech develops more quickly than it would otherwise have developed (Bodine & Beukelman 1991, Van Tatenhove 1987). Beukelman and Mirenda (1998) assert that "the goal of AAC is to support the child's attempts to communicate successfully until such time as (hopefully) speech is adequate to meet ongoing communication needs."

Appropriate Populations

While there may be particular groups of children for whom AAC is a particularly good choice, the American Speech-Language-Hearing Association (ASHA) defines the population who may benefit from AAC as "those for whom gestural, speech, and/or written communication is temporarily or permanently inadequate to meet all of their communication needs. For those individuals, hearing impairment is not the primary cause for the communication impairment. Although some individuals may be able to produce a limited amount of speech, it is inadequate to meet their varied communication needs. Numerous terms that were initially used in the field but are now rarely mentioned include *speechless, nonoral, nonvocal, nonverbal,* and *aphonic*" (ASHA 1991).

Given this definition, the majority of the toddlers who receive services from speech-language pathologists (SLPs) are good candidates for AAC due to language delays or speech disorders that limit their abilities to meet their communication needs. Some of the children who receive services from the SLP may be permanently unable to use speech to communicate. These children may continue to need an alternative communication system later in life. However, many of the children will eventually establish verbal communication and will therefore need an augmentative system for a relatively short time.

The most common congenital causes of the inability to speak without adaptive assistance are mental retardation, cerebral palsy, autism, and developmental apraxia of speech (Mirenda & Mathy-Laikko 1989). It has been estimated that between 8 and 12 persons per 1000 experience severe communication impairments that require AAC (Beukelman & Ansel 1995). (See Chapter 4 for more details regarding medical diagnoses that predispose children to language delays.)

Types of Augmentative Communication

Communication systems may be unaided, which means that external objects are not required. Communication systems may also be aided, which involves the use of physical objects.

Examples of Unaided Communication	Examples of Aided Communication
gestures body language sign language vocalizations speech	real objects miniature objects photographs line drawings pictorial symbols orthographic symbols (i.e., writing)

Among young children, sign language (an unaided system) and pictures (an aided system) have been shown to be effective for establishing a means of communication. Additionally, some basic communication devices and adapted toys may be beneficial for young children.

Sign Language

The gestural system that comprises sign language is as important as sounds are for spoken language (Apel & Masterson 2001). Sign language is clearly an important means of communication for children with hearing impairments. In addition, children who hear have been able to use simple signs to communicate their needs to their deaf parents when they were less than one year of age (Riekehof 1987). Further, Riekehof reports that using signs at an early age may decrease the frustration that frequently accompanies the communication barrier of deafness. Using this rationale, signs are also beneficial for children who experience frustration as a result of a language delay or speech disorder.

Providing a child with a way to communicate via signs allows the child to assert some control in meeting his wants and needs. This is important as it has been shown that people who were frequently exposed to situations over which they controlled their fate were more resistant to developing helpless behavior (Seligman 1975). Children with communication impairments are indeed at risk for developing learned helplessness, whereby they may become very passive and may give up attempts to communicate because adults anticipate, often incorrectly, the children's needs (Ballinger 1999).

In choosing the signs to teach children, the vocabulary must be customized for each child based on his needs. To ensure successful communication, it is critical that the child has access to the right vocabulary (Light & Binger 1998). (Note: Chapter 9, pages 92–94, contains information about developing a core lexicon.) In order to choose the most important vocabulary items, caregivers should be involved in the vocabulary selection. Suggested questions to ask caregivers to help develop appropriate vocabulary include the following.

- Which family members does your child interact with regularly?
- What other people does your child see regularly?
- If your family has pets, what type of animals are they?
- What are some of your child's favorite foods?
- What does your child like to drink?
- What toys does your child play with the most?
- What are some activities that your child does regularly?
- Are there other things you would like your child to tell you (e.g., pain, anger, hunger, thirst)?

Some core vocabulary suggestions are listed in the box on the next page. They are divided by general themes. Illustrations of the signs for these words are in Appendix 11B (pages 137–142). The cards in this kit also include the illustrations as well as written descriptions on how to make the signs. The core vocabulary was compiled from *The Comprehensive Signed English Dictionary* (Bornstein et al. 1983), *Signing: How to Speak with Your Hands* (Costello 1983), and *The Joy of Signing*, 2nd ed. (Riekehof 1987). With children in this age group, it is important to remember that they may not have the fine motor coordination to perform the signs exactly. Therefore, approximations of the signs should be accepted and reinforced.

Chapter 11: Augmentative and Alternative Communication

Possible Vocabulary Words for Signing

Alphabet

Numbers
1-10

Animals/Pets
bear
bird
bunny
cat
dog
horse

Family
Mommy
Daddy
baby
Grandma
Grandpa
(names for the child,
  family members,
  caregivers, etc.)

Play Time
ball
block
bubbles
car
drop
hug
kick
kiss
play
pull
push
ride
shake

Mealtime Snacks
apple
cookie
cracker
drink
eat
juice
milk
water

Requesting
big
come
down
finished/all done/all gone
give
go
help
I/me
little
mad
more
my/mine
night-night
no
please
stop
up
want
yes
you/your

Pictures

Pictures of objects and activities may also be a method for children to communicate their wants and needs. Pictures are among many symbol systems that may be used in AAC. As previously noted, pictures are considered to be an aided communication system. A consideration that is of importance with all AAC users, but that may have more importance with this young population, is the iconicity of the symbols. Glennen and DeCoste (1997) refer to iconicity as the "guessability of symbols." More specifically, *iconicity* is the degree that the sign or symbol visually resembles or suggests what the symbol refers to (Bloomberg et al. 1990, Dunham 1989, Fuller & Lloyd 1991, McEwen & Lloyd 1990, Mizuko 1987, Orlansky & Bonvillian 1984, Sevcik et al. 1991).

Mirenda and Locke (1989) described a symbol hierarchy from easiest (most guessable) to hardest (least guessable) in terms of iconicity. This hierarchy follows:

- objects
- color photographs
- black and white photographs
- miniature objects
- black and white line drawings
- Blissymbols (a picture language that combines 100 basic elements for meaning)
- traditional orthography (i.e., writing)

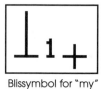

Blissymbol for "my"

Symbols are learned more easily and quickly when symbols are more iconic (Clark 1981, Yovetich & Young 1988). Therefore, the birth-to-three population will benefit more from use of symbols that more clearly represent the item, such as photographs or miniature objects. Further, it has been shown that by 24 months of age, children see photographs as symbols for the objects depicted (Mirenda & Locke 1989). Because of this finding and the notion that the meanings of symbols must be known to both of the communication partners (Glennen & DeCoste 1997), it is recommended to use photographs when implementing an AAC system that uses pictures in early intervention services. Color photographs may be best because they are more iconic than black and white photographs. These photographs may be used for picture exchange or for creating communication boards for this population.

Picture exchange

The *Picture Exchange Communication System* (PECS) is an approach that has been used to establish symbolic communication for individuals with autism (Bondy & Frost 1993). With picture exchange, a picture symbol is handed to a communication partner in exchange for a desired item or action. This system allows the user to begin to learn how to use symbols to manipulate specific outcomes in the environment and promotes communication as a social exchange (Glennen & DeCoste 1997). This interactive picture exchange may help the child transition to a less-interactive, two-dimensional communication display in which the child points to picture symbols to indicate his desire but does not have to hand anything to the communication partner.

Communication boards

In general, communication boards combine the alphabet, words, and/or pictures to which the user points as a means of expressive communication. For the birth-to-three population, communication boards are usually comprised of pictures. Because each picture on a communication board generally has a single meaning, a large number of symbols are needed. Therefore, it may be beneficial to create individualized, themed communication boards (e.g., foods, toys, clothes). The number of pictures that can be put on the communication board so it may be effectively used by the child is dependent on the child's skills. Some children may be able to choose between only two pictures, while others may be able to select from 20 or more pictures.

It may be beneficial to use Velcro to attach pictures to the communication board. Then the communication board can be customized to accommodate particular situations such as limiting choices to those available at the time. For example, parents can remove pictures of items as needed (e.g., remove the picture of bananas from the food communication board when the last banana is eaten).

Low technology communication devices

While pictures may be used to create communication boards or communication books, there are additional low technology options for communication and play. Two options that may be used with the birth-to-three population are eye gaze systems and switches. These strategies are relatively low in cost and are generally easy to use. Low technology options may be used to provide words or picture symbols that are specific to each day's activities.

Eye gaze systems

Eye gaze is the use of eye movements to point to objects or pictures. This option may be particularly beneficial for a child with mobility limitations. A special clear Plexiglas board known as an E-Tran may be used to affix symbols for eye gaze (Glennen & DeCoste 1997). Crestwood Communication Aids, Inc. has different versions of Plexiglas boards available which can be used for pictures, words, letters, and/or objects.

Communication partners may also hold pictures or objects in front of the child so that the child looks at the pictures or objects. Depending on the child's ability, it may be necessary to place objects or pictures vertically so that the child looks either up or down to make a selection, or horizontally so the child looks to the right or left. When eye gaze is used, the size of the symbols should be appropriate for the child's visual acuity.

Switches

A variety of switches is available. One of the main considerations in choosing a switch is determining the body movement necessary to activate the switch. Other considerations include the amount of pressure needed and the length of time required to activate the switch. Switches may be used to activate a toy or piece of equipment such as a tape recorder. Some switches may be used to record messages. Some that record messages allow a single message to be recorded, whereas others are multi-step and allow a scripted sequence to be recorded. Switches that may be useful for the birth-to-three population include AbleNet's *Big Red* switch, *Jelly Bean* switch, or *BIGmack* communicator.

Introducing AAC

Once a decision has been made to attempt use of an AAC system, there are several considerations regarding how to introduce the symbols to the child. Each case will be different due to medical diagnoses, cognitive abilities, mobility concerns, speech and language diagnoses, and other issues (e.g., child's communication needs at home vs. at daycare). Remember that a communication system is not a static entity. It should be viewed as a dynamic system. As the child's comprehension and vocabulary change, you will make revisions to the system.

Hoge and Newsome (2001) provide some guidelines for choosing an AAC system for individuals with severe developmental delays and for teaching targeted skills. Some of their suggestions are briefly outlined below.

1. **Intervention issues**

    - Access/Motor capabilities
      It is paramount for the child to have access to the communication system or device throughout the day in order to effectively use it. Children with motor difficulties may have additional considerations regarding positioning to use the AAC system.

If sign language/gestures are the AAC of choice, positioning may be less of an issue than if pictures or a device are being used. If pictures are being used, different boards or sets of pictures should be created based on what is needed for a particular situation. For example, pictures needed in the kitchen to request food and drinks are different from pictures the child needs in his room to request toys. A solution may be to have picture boards hanging on the refrigerator and on the closet door in the child's room (as well as in appropriate places for other situations). Pictures can be attached to the boards using Velcro so that they may be moved as needed, either to use in different situations or if the item the picture represents becomes unavailable.

- Reinforcers
It is essential to find something that the child enjoys so that he can be taught to ask for what he wants. Without an appropriate reinforcer, the child will not be motivated to participate in tasks to improve communication. Reinforcers may be determined through observation and interviews with caregivers. However, there may also be time when reinforcers are not known because the child is a passive observer. If the child does not overtly indicate what he likes, subtle cues may be obtained from facial expressions or body postures.

- Staff/Caregiver training
Education may be needed to lessen the caregivers' hesitation of using AAC as they may view these methods as relinquishing the pursuit of verbal speech. Caregivers should also be trained regarding strategies to facilitate use of communication to meet the child's needs, such as waiting for the child to use the sign/gesture/picture or structuring the environment to elicit communication. Frequently caregivers understand and anticipate what the child wants, and ultimately meet the need of the child before a communication attempt is made.

2. **Teaching targeted skills**

    - Cause/Effect
    If the child does not understand the relationship between cause and effect, this should be the first skill taught in order to develop further communication skills. Some activities in the *Activities Book* address cause and effect (e.g., P19a, P19b). Initially, intervention may require use of hand-over-hand assistance with the child to touch the targeted symbol or to perform the sign/gesture. The reinforcer should then be given to the child within three seconds so he can make the connection between the two (Korsten et al. 1993).

    - Turn taking
    If a child is not taking turns in nonverbal activities, it will be difficult to teach verbal turn taking because verbal communication is more abstract than the nonverbal turn taking that is typically developed in early infancy. While a child may not initially communicate with intent (e.g., randomly touches a switch with a recorded message such as "Come read to me"),

the response he gets when he does touch the switch may cause him to initiate turns and communication. For example, if the caregiver reinforces the child's request, the child may begin to associate the action of touching the switch with the consequence of being read to. After initial turns, communication partners can wait for the child to activate a switch, point to a picture, etc. to make the next request. This teaches the child that he is able to initiate interactions with others. He then may be willing to take another turn to request a different object or comment on an object.

- Discriminating Between Choices
  Initially a single symbol may be presented until the child touches it (or looks at it if using eye gaze). Once a response is established, a choice between two items should be offered. If successful, the number of choices may be increased. If unsuccessful, it may be necessary to provide alternative choices such as preferred and non-preferred choices (e.g., cookie vs. cauliflower) or the desired item and a blank choice. It may also be necessary to change the stimulus (e.g., changing from presenting photographs alone to pairing photographs with objects).

Speech with Tracheostomy

Children with tracheostomies may require speech and language therapy to develop an early communication system and to establish vocalizations. Methods for establishing vocalizations are described on the next page. AAC options may include sign language, picture boards, and artificial speech via an electrolarynx. Sign language and pictures were described previously in this chapter. See Chapter 4 (pages 43–44) for additional information on tracheostomies.

Vocal production

Because tracheostomies are placed in the trachea below the level of the vocal folds, patients with tracheostomies are unable to achieve voicing without allowing the air to flow up through vocal cords. Voicing may be achieved in a number of ways including finger occlusion, placement of a speaking valve, and the minimal leak technique. While a fenestrated tracheostomy cannula (tracheostomy cannula with holes in it) may be used with some adult clients to achieve voicing, this is not recommended for use with infants as it may cause weakening of the tracheal wall (Simon & McGowan 1989). Before attempting any method to achieve vocal production, a physician's order should be obtained. In addition, the SLP should have demonstrated competency in working with children with tracheostomies.

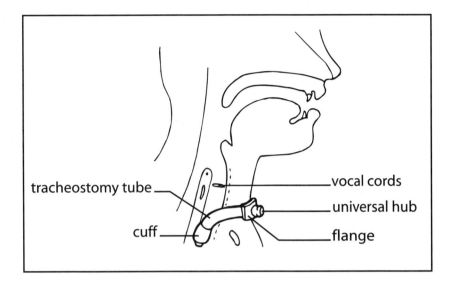

- Finger occlusion
  If present, the tracheostomy cuff is deflated. A finger is placed over the cannula intermittently for 1 to 3 seconds. This may be done by the clinician (with a gloved finger), parent, or the child. Children have been shown to independently occlude their tracheostomies by 1 to 2 years of age (Simon & McGowan 1989). However, this method is not as sanitary as other techniques.

- Speaking valve
  Speaking valves are one-way valves that allow air to flow into the tracheostomy, up through the vocal cords, and out the mouth. These valves are used only when the tracheostomy cuff (if present) is completely deflated.

  One type of speaking valve that may be used both on and off a ventilator is the Passy-Muir Tracheostomy Speaking Valve. While not all patients are able to tolerate wearing a Passy-Muir valve, for young children who are able to tolerate the valve, there may be extraordinary benefits in establishing vocal communication and facilitating cognitive and language development. Passy-Muir valves may also improve the physiological status of a baby with a tracheostomy to improve swallowing function (Abraham 2003).

- Minimal leak
  This technique involves slightly deflating the cuff of the tracheostomy. Some air then travels around the partially deflated cuff through the vocal folds and allows the child to produce some phonation.

  Factors that may prevent the child from achieving voicing include a tight-fitting cannula and subglottic stenosis (i.e., narrowing of the airway below the larynx). Additionally, fluctuations in the child's vocalizations may occur when there are changes in the cannula size, airway, or ventilator settings.

Non-vocal communication systems

When consistent vocalizations are not achieved, it is necessary to establish an alternative means of communication. These systems may include any combination of the following:

- signs/gestures
- pictures
- communication devices
- electrolarynx

Previous sections of this chapter discuss use of signs/gestures, pictures, and communication devices. An electrolarynx is used for artificial speech and may be helpful for the child to approximate normal speech movements even when verbalizations are absent or intermittent.

Summary

While there are numerous considerations for implementing AAC strategies, there are many potential benefits with such systems. For the birth-to-three population, early intervention and introduction of AAC may provide a child with the ability to make his wants and needs known through alternative means. AAC may also be used to facilitate verbal speech production. Both outcomes decrease chances of developing learned helplessness. Systems that may be particularly useful for the birth-to-three population are sign language, picture systems, low technology devices, and toys with adapted switches to teach cause/effect. Special equipment may also be needed for children with tracheostomies. Regardless of the system used, the child's family should be involved in order to choose the most appropriate vocabulary. Further, intervention should address functional needs and should be individualized for each child.

Resources

Web Sites

AAC Intervention.com
Augmentative/Alternative Communication
Intervention Products & Presentations
www.aacintervention.com

ASHA Web Site for Special Interest Division 12, Augmentative and Alternative Communication.
www.asha.org/about/membership/certification/divs/div_12.htm

Augmentative and Alternative Communication (AAC) Connecting Young Kids (YAACK)
http://aac.unl.edu/yaack/index.html

Augmentative Communication, Inc.
www.augcominc.com

Augmentative Communication On-Line Users Group (ACOLUG) LISTSERV
http://disabilities.temple.edu/programs/assistive/acolug

The International Society for Augmentative and Alternative Communication (ISAAC)
www.isaac-online.org

The Parent Advocacy Coalition for Educational Rights (PACER)
www.pacer.org

Books

Expanded Songs in Sign
S. H. Collins & K. Kifer (Illustrator) 1998

Family and Community
J. Schneider, K. Kifer (Illustrator), &
S. H. Collins 1999

Foods
S. H. Collins, K. Kifer (Illustrator), & J. Phillips (Designer) 2001

Fruits & Vegetables
K. Kifer (Illustrator) & S. H. Collins 1997

Handbook of Augmentative and Alternative Communication
S. L. Glennen & D. C. DeCoste 1996/1997

Holidays & Celebrations
S. H. Collins, K. Kifer, (Illustrator), & J. Schneider 1999

More Simple Signs
C. Wheeler 1998

Pets, Animals, & Creatures
J. Phillips (Illustrator), K. Kifer (Illustrator),
M. Krasnik (Illustrator), & S. H. Collins 2001

Signs for Me: Basic Sign Vocabulary for Children, Parents & Teachers
B. Bahan & J. Dannis 1990

Simple Signs
C. Wheeler 1997

Videos

Baby See'n Sign 2001
Baby Signs 2001
Blues Clues—All Kinds of Signs 2001
Sign With Me 2000
Talking Hands: A Sign Language Video for Children 2000
We Sign: ABC 2001
We Sign: Animals 2001
We Sign: Babies and Toddlers 2002
We Sign: Colors 2001
We Sign: Patriotic Songs 2002
We Sign: Play Time 2003
We Sign: Rhymes 2001

continued on next page

Appendix 11A

Manufacturers

Abilitations
One Sportime Way
Atlanta, GA 30340
1-800-850-8603
www.abilitations.com

Ablenet
1081 Tenth Avenue SE
Minneapolis, MN 55414-1312
1-800-322-0956
www.ablenetinc.com

Adam Lab
55 East Long Lake Road, Suite 337
Troy, MI 48085
(248) 362-9603
www.adamlab.com

Attainment Company
P.O. Box 930160
Verona, WI 35393
1-800-327-4269
www.attainmentcompany.com

Crestwood Communications Aids, Inc.
6625 North Sidney Place
Milwaukee, WI 53209
(414) 352-5678
www.communicationaids.com

Passy-Muir, Inc.
PMB 273
4521 Campus Drive
Irvine, CA 92612
1-800-634-5397
www.passy-muir.com

PRO-Ed, Inc.
8700 Shoal Creek Blvd.
Austin, TX 78757
1-800-897-3202
www.proedinc.com

Appendix 11B

Suggested Vocabulary Words in Sign Language

The words are listed in alphabetical order. However, because many signs are made holding the hands in the shape of letters or numbers, pictures of the signs for letters in the alphabet and the numbers 1 through 10 are given first. It may be necessary to adapt some signs to meet the child's abilities. Therefore, approximations may be accepted as correct productions of the sign. Additionally, alternate representations may be used (e.g., *mad* may be represented with a foot stomp or a "mad" facial expression). If approximations or alternates are used, all caregivers, teachers, and others who use signs with the child should be advised. (Note: When signing names for the child, family members, caregivers, etc., frequently the first letter of the person's name is signed in front of the chest.)

Alphabet

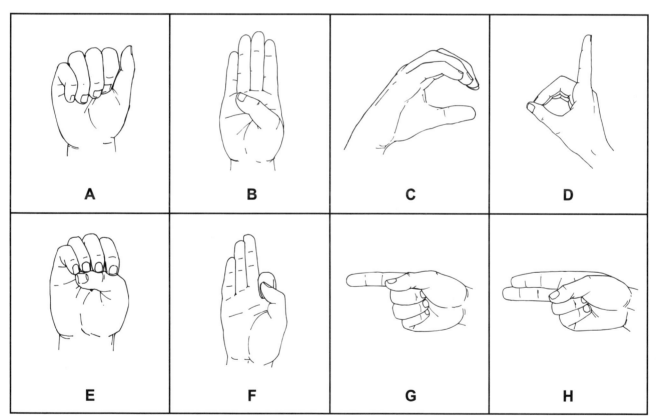

continued on next page

Appendix 11B

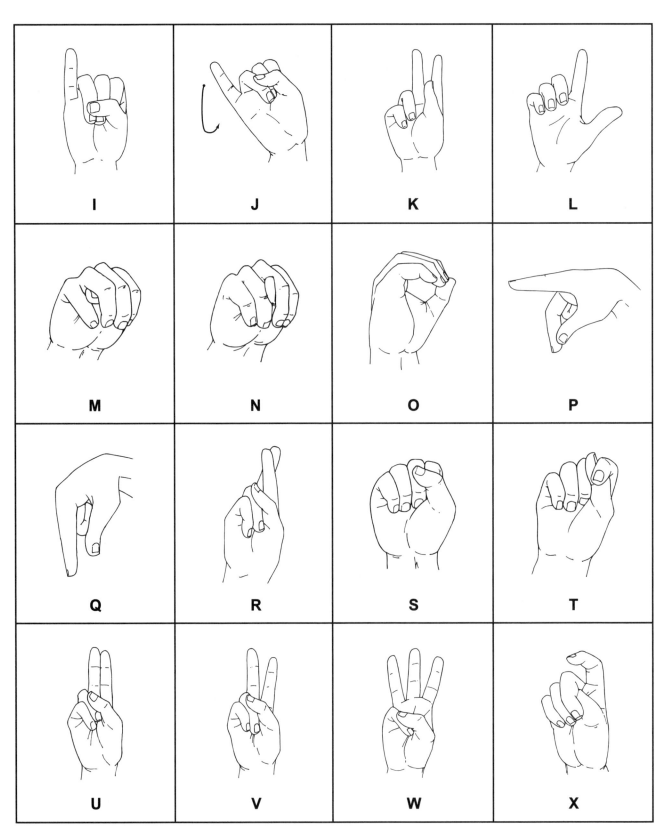

continued on next page

Appendix 11B

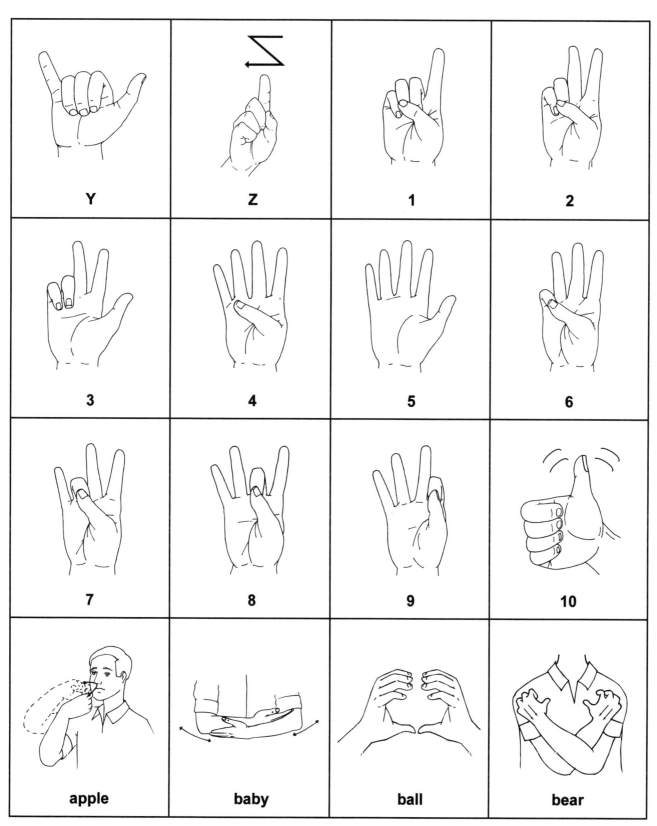

continued on next page

Appendix 11B

Therapy Guide
The Early Intervention Kit

Appendix 11B

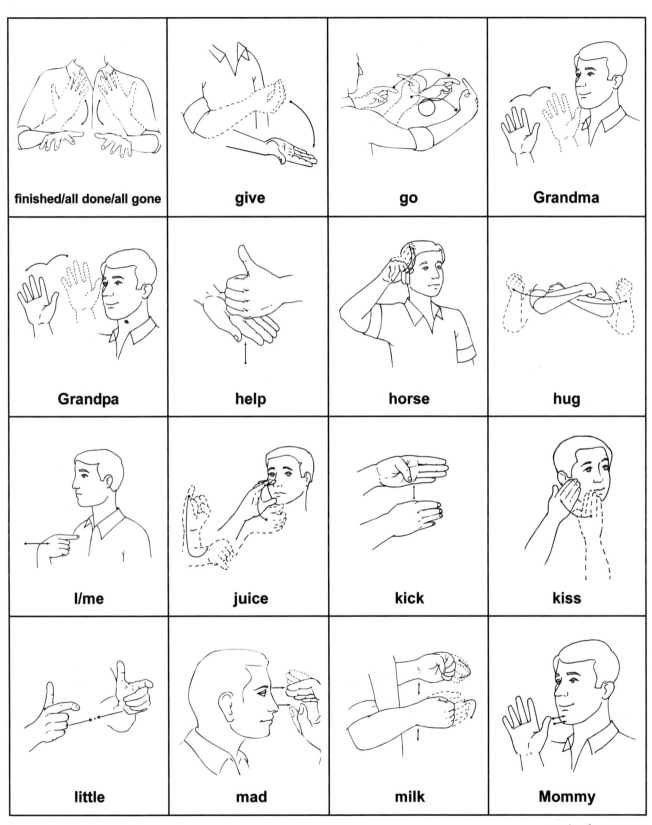

continued on next page

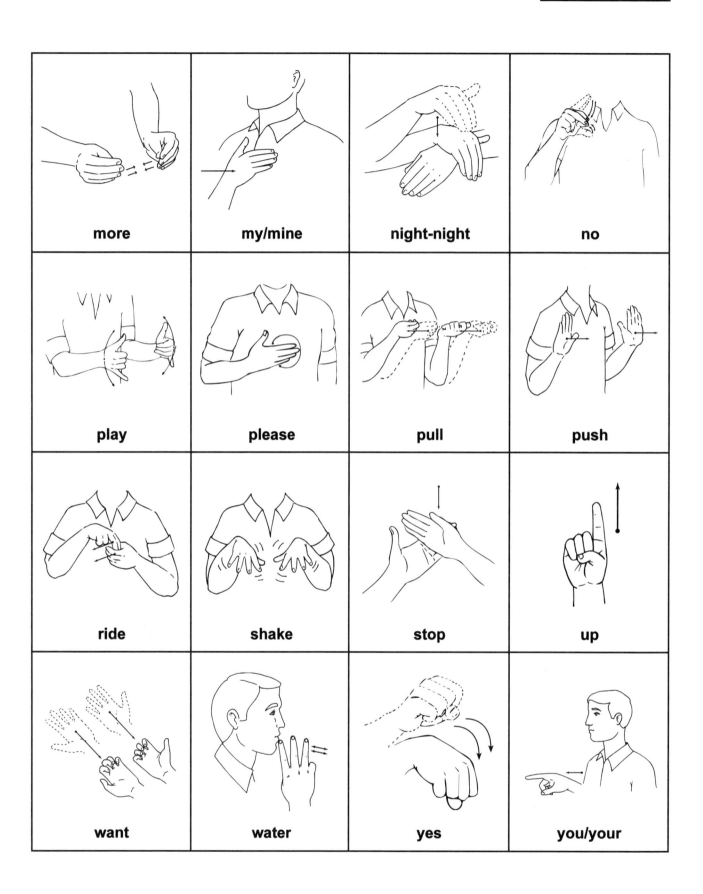

Chapter 12

Documentation

In all areas of practice for speech-language pathologists, documenting what you do is as important as doing it. When documenting services for the birth-to-three population, there are some significant differences in the format and forms used, as well as in the language used on those forms. Mastering these differences will help you become more efficient in the provision of services and spend less time on paperwork.

Discipline-Specific Assessment

You are responsible for writing an assessment report to summarize your findings. As mentioned in Chapter 2, this report is called an *assessment*, not an *evaluation*. The report should be organized in sections with headers that capture the information required for the Individualized Family Service Plan (IFSP). A sample speech and language assessment is provided in Appendix 12A, pages 157–159. Suggested headers for the assessment include:

Pertinent medical history
Describe any medical history specifically related to the communication and/or swallowing problem you are assessing.

Hearing
Children under three cannot reliably be screened with pure tones by the SLP, so this section should contain observations about the child's hearing acuity, information from the newborn infant hearing screening if one was done, and any information from an audiologic evaluation.

State of health
Describe any ongoing medical problems that may have an impact on the child's development (e.g., recent bout of otitis media, taking medication for a seizure disorder).

Level of response
Was the child alert and responsive during the assessment or did you have to obtain most of the information from the caregiver? Was the child responding typically during the assessment? For instance, sometimes a child doesn't follow any directions for the clinician, but the mom gives examples of things that the child does to follow directions. Or a child may be very fussy during the assessment because of being sick or tired. On the other hand, sometimes parents will notice the child doing things during the assessment that they don't usually see at home.

Persons present
Who supplied the background information and answered questions about the child's abilities? Who else was present and interacting with the child?

Sources/measures used
It is required that more than one type of measure be used to obtain information about the child's abilities.

_____ Behavioral checklist _____

_____ Standardized tests _____

_____ Parent interview

_____ Criterion-referenced instrument _____

_____ Observation _____

Concerns
List what the caregiver describes as concerns. It is helpful to use the language the caregiver uses. For example, "Gray's mother is worried that he does not seem to know the names of toys he plays with" or "Shanita's grandmother is worried that Shanita does not answer when asked what she wants to eat." If the family has trouble verbalizing concerns, ask questions to help them focus their thoughts.

Priorities
Of the concerns listed, have the caregiver prioritize what she would like therapy to address. You can reword these as needed. For example, Shanita's grandmother has indicated she wants Shanita to answer when asked what she wants to eat. You might list this as: "Shanita's grandmother wants her to be able to answer simple 'what' questions." You may need to help the caregiver understand that some prerequisite skills need to be met in order to address a given priority. For example, perhaps Shanita does not know the names of the foods offered and needs to increase receptive understanding and expressive use of food and drink words.

Priorities can also include things such as working around the parent's work or school schedule, therapy to be conducted at daycare, Dad wants to participate in sessions, etc. For example, "Gray will be seen 3X a month at his mother's house and 1X a month at his father's house."

Strengths
List strengths that you observed during your assessment. This can include skills the child exhibited and things such as how well the child attended, if the child seemed alert, and that the parents are supportive and eager to learn.

Needs
These are the deficit areas you identified during your assessment.

Emerging skills
These are skills the child exhibits on an inconsistent basis. Listing emerging skills is important because this gives you a starting point in therapy.

Materials and equipment to support development
List toys and books that would be good for the child to develop language skills (e.g., books with large colorful pictures, objects that can be taken apart and put back together). For feeding/swallowing, you might recommend certain utensils.

Comments
Make a few summary statements of the child's present level in areas assessed.

Parent education
State that the assessment results were discussed with the parent and what the parents said about the results. Describe any questions you addressed.

Diagnosis
Give a diagnosis in all assessed areas that show deficits.

Eligibility
Clearly state if the child qualifies for the early intervention services based on your state's guidelines.

Rationale
If the child is eligible for early intervention services, provide a rationale for eligibility (e.g., The child qualifies because her expressive language skills are more than two standard deviations below the mean).

Recommend services be provided in natural environment? If *no*, provide the rationale.
As described in Chapter 2, most states are urging (and some requiring) that services be provided in the natural environment. If services are to be provided in a clinical setting instead, a strong rationale must be given.

Recommendations
This might include any other assessments (e.g., audiological evaluation, referral to medical specialty) you recommend as well as whether you are recommending speech-language and/or feeding/swallowing therapy. The frequency and intensity of therapy will be determined later by the team.

Strategies and activities for parent to implement
In keeping with the focus on the parent, some activities should be chosen during which the caregiver can immediately begin to address the child's needs. Specific strategies to use during those activities should be explained. (See the *Activities Book* for the parent handout, *Strategies to Facilitate Communication*, pages 159–161.)

Discipline-Specific Treatment Plan

Depending on the agency providing the services, a discipline-specific treatment plan may be required. This will be worded in language familiar to the SLP, with long-term and short-term goals and treatment objectives. Some agencies may not require any paperwork other than the IFSP to list the goals. A sample treatment plan can be found in Appendix 12B, page 160.

Chapter 12: Documentation

Individualized Family Service Plan (IFSP)

The law requires that an IFSP be developed for each family of an eligible child. The IFSP is developed and completed by the multidisciplinary team members including the child's parents. The service coordinator is responsible for making sure the IFSP is implemented and for coordinating services among agencies. A sample IFSP form can be found in Appendix 12C (pages 161–163). Noonan and McCormick (1993) summarize what must be included in the IFSP:

a. a statement of the child's present level of functioning in cognitive development, communication development, social or emotional development, physical development, and adaptive development

b. a statement of the family's concerns, priorities, and resources

c. a statement of expected intervention outcomes, including criteria, procedures, and timelines

d. a description of the services that the child and family need, including method, frequency, and intensity

e. a statement of the natural environments in which early intervention services will be provided

f. projected dates for initiation of services and expected duration

g. the name of the service coordinator who will be responsible for implementing the plan and coordinating with other agencies

h. the procedure to insure successful transition from infant services to preschool programs

The IFSP must be reviewed every six months and its appropriateness evaluated once a year. The IFSP must also be fully explained to the parents so they can provide written consent.

Developing an IFSP presents some challenges because the wording required is quite different from that used in an IEP or in a medically-based report. Instead of terms like *deficits* and *disorders*, the plan includes language about a family's resources, priorities, and concerns. Specific terminology is included to describe how the parents will use strategies and activities to achieve goals.

The IFSP also serves as your written form of authorization for treatment (similar to receiving pre-authorization from an insurance company or having the parent of a school-age child sign an IEP). You must pay close attention to the dates listed on the IFSP, and not begin services before the start date nor continue services past the stop date.

Progress note for IFSP meeting

You may be required to write a progress note to document your attendance at the IFSP meeting. Having a note that already contains most of the essential information can save time. Then you need only to write in additional information that is discussed. A progress note designed for use at an IFSP meeting can be found in Appendix 12D, page 164.

Chapter 12: Documentation

Development of outcomes

The final phase of the IFSP process is the meeting of all the team members with the caregivers. All of the assessment information is reviewed and outcomes statements are developed. These outcomes statements must be focused on what the family wants the child to achieve.

Noonan and McCormick (1993) describe an effective way to help families identify potential outcomes/goals for the child. Have the parents complete the first four columns of a typical weekday and typical weekend schedule to describe the activities the child is engaged in, what the child does, and what the caregivers do. (See Figure 12-1 below.) This format clearly shows opportunities for skill development in activities of daily living. The team then converts these opportunities for skill development into potential child outcomes and lists them in the fifth column. The final column includes family strategies (changes in family behavior that will help the child achieve the goal). Columns five and six should be discussed by the team. (Note: A blank version of this form can be found in Appendix 12E, page 165.) This form will also help you complete the *Strategies/Activities* section of the IFSP. (See Appendix 12C, pages 162–163.)

Developing Outcomes from Daily Activities

Columns 1–4 completed by family   Columns 5 and 6 completed by team

Time	Activity	What the child does	What the caregiver does	Potential child outcome/goal	Potential family member strategy
6:30	Wake up	Nicholas cries.	Mom usually gets up, changes his diaper, and puts him in his swing.	Nicholas will use the word "Mom" to call for attention; Nicholas will reach out arms to be picked up.	Mom will talk about what she is doing with Nicholas, particularly teaching action words: *get up*, *change*, *swing*.
7:30	Rest of family up and breakfast is prepared	Nicholas watches from his swing.	Mom cooks, brother turns on TV, Dad fixes bottle and warms cereal.	Nicholas will vocalize to initiate interactions.	Mom will talk about what she is doing; Brother will keep TV off and talk to Nicholas.
7:45	Eating breakfast	Nicholas is placed in his high chair.	Dad feeds Nicholas.	Nicholas will put up arms to be taken from swing to be put in high chair; Nicholas will imitate "mmm" with bites of food; Nicholas will use sign for "more" to get more bites.	Dad will model "mmm" for bites of food; Dad will wait for Nicholas to sign "more" before giving next bite.
8:15	Dressing	Nicholas lies on his back or sits supported.	Mom dresses Nicholas.	Nicholas will point to his head and his feet.	Mom will identify body parts as she dresses Nicholas; Mom will label clothes.

Figure 12-1   Adapted from Noonan & McCormick 1993

Skills from different domains for the same outcome/goal

The multidisciplinary nature of early intervention lends itself to identifying goals/outcomes that can be addressed by more than one discipline. For example, perhaps the parents' goal is for the child to play with an older sibling in a game such as rolling a ball back and forth. The physical therapist might need to address the child's sitting balance, the occupational therapist would address the child's fine motor skills to grasp the ball, and the SLP would address the child's use of a gesture or word to indicate she wants the ball.

The example of a daily schedule on page 147 only incorporates communication goals but could easily be used by other members of the team to incorporate their goals. See Figure 12-2 for addition of fine and gross motor goals to the schedule. These are listed in italics.

Time	Activity	What the child does	What the caregiver does	Potential child outcome/goal	Potential family member strategy
6:30	Wake up	Nicholas cries.	Mom usually gets him up, changes his diaper, and puts him in his swing.	Nicholas will use the word "Mom" to call for attention. Nicholas will reach out arms to be picked up. *Nicholas will pull to sit after diaper change.*	Mom will talk about what she is doing with Nicholas, particularly teaching action words: *get up, change, swing*. *Mom will assist with pull to sit with hand behind Nicholas' back.*
7:30	Rest of family up and breakfast is prepared	Nicholas watches from his swing.	Mom cooks, brother turns on TV, Dad fixes bottle and warms cereal.	Nicholas will vocalize to initiate interactions.	Mom will talk about what she is doing. Brother will keep TV off and talk to Nicholas. *Dad will perform sensory stimulation activities*
7:45	Eating breakfast	Nicholas is placed in his high chair.	Dad feeds Nicholas.	Nicholas will put up arms to be taken from swing to be put in high chair. Nicholas will imitate "mmm" with bites of food. Nicholas will use sign for "more" to get more bites. *Nicholas will grasp spoon and feed himself a few bites.*	Dad will model "mmm" for bites of food. Dad will wait for Nicholas to sign "more" before giving next bite. *Dad will use hand over hand assist as needed with spoon feeding.*
8:15	Dressing	Nicholas lies on his back or sits supported.	Mom dresses Nicholas.	Nicholas will point to his head and his feet. *Nicholas will pull to sit after being dressed.*	Mom will identify body parts as she dresses Nicholas; Mom will label clothes. *Mom will assist with pull to sit.*

Figure 12-2

These outcomes are written in the family's wording, not in the words of professionals. For example, the family may want the child to "use words instead of grunting and pointing to communicate." You might have worded it as "child will increase single word vocabulary to name things in environment to request an object or an action."

Strategies and activities

In addition to child/family outcomes, the IFSP will include strategies, activities, and practical suggestions to meet the outcomes. Although often listed in the same column, strategies and activities are different. *Strategies* are facilitating techniques the family can use to help achieve the outcome. *Activities* are activities of daily living during which the strategies can be employed. Strategies for communication development include:

expansion	providing prompts
forgetfulness	supplementing verbal speech with picture stimuli
giving choices	questioning
guided learning	sabotage
imitation	self-talk
let the child lead	sign language
modeling	supplementing verbal speech with signs/gestures
novelty	using object with/instead of word
out of reach	using touch cue with the sound
parallel talk	violating expectations
paraphrasing	wait and see
picture stimuli	withholding an object to get the desired response
piece-by-piece	

For more complete description of these strategies, see pages 159–161 in the *Activities Book*.

Long-term and short-term goals

You must analyze the caregivers' desired outcomes/goals for the child and determine what long-term and short-term goals will need to be met in order to reach each desired outcome. For example, if the parents want the child to stop screaming when she can't reach something on the counter, you determine that the child will need to improve her expressive language skills (long-term goal) and will need to learn to use single words to request an object (short-term goal). She may also need to improve receptive language (long-term goal) and increase her understanding of questions (short-term goal). In addition, she may need to improve sound production (long-term goal) and specifically increase use of target final consonants (short-term goal). All of these short-term goals may need to be accomplished in order to help the child achieve the parents' desired outcome.

A master list of long-term and short-term goals is listed on the next page.

Chapter 12: Documentation

Long- and Short-term Goals for Pre-linguistic Skills, Receptive Language Skills, Expressive Language Skills, and Sound Production Development

Pre-linguistic Skills

Long-term goal: The child will be able to maintain attention to stimuli and interact with objects and people appropriately.

Short-term goals:
PG1 The child will make and maintain eye contact/visual contact with object/picture/person.
PG2 The child will imitate non-vocal actions.
PG3 The child will imitate vocalizations.
PG4 The child will utilize objects (or imaginary objects) in appropriate play/self-care.
PG5 The child will engage in turn-taking routines.
PG6 The child will demonstrate object permanence.
PG7 The child will respond with appropriate gesture/action to sound, speech, and/or gesture.
PG8 The child will initiate use of appropriate gesture to obtain desired effect.
PG9 The child will demonstrate other problem-solving skills.

Receptive Language Skills

Long-term goal: The child will exhibit optimal receptive language skills.

Short-term goals:
RG1 The child will respond to speech.
RG2 The child will understand single words from a variety of word classes.
RG3 The child will follow simple one-step commands accompanied by gestures/context clues.
RG4 The child will follow simple one-step commands without gesture/context support.
RG5 The child will follow two-step (and three-step) commands.
RG6 The child will understand simple questions.

Expressive Language Skills

Long-term goal: The child will exhibit optimal expressive language skills.

Short-term goals:
EG1 The child will increase imitation of vocalizations of non-speech sounds, speech sounds, and sound sequences.
EG2 The child will increase imitation of words.
EG3 The child will increase spontaneous use of vocalizations of non-speech sounds, speech sounds, and sound sequences.
EG4 The child will increase spontaneous use of single words.
EG5 The child will increase spontaneous use of word combinations.

Sound Production Development

Long-term goal: The child will speak intelligibly as compared to developmental age peers.

Short-term goals:
SG1 The child will imitate target consonants in isolation.
SG2 The child will imitate target consonants in words.
SG3 The child will produce target consonants in words.
SG4 The child will imitate target vowels in isolation.
SG5 The child will imitate target vowels in words.
SG6 The child will produce target vowels in words.
SG7 The child will produce target consonants in connected speech.
SG8 The child will produce target vowels in connected speech.
SG9 The child will demonstrate mastery of phonological patterns.

Treatment objectives

After selecting appropriate long-term and short-term goals, more specific and measurable treatment objectives should be selected. These specific, measurable treatment objectives are often needed on a treatment plan for individual disciplines. The objectives should have three essential components (Noonan & McCormick 1993):

1. Conditions under which the skill is to be performed are specified (e.g., *while Jonita is in the bathtub*).

2. The skill is stated in observable, measurable terms (e.g., *Jonita will use single words to request toys for the tub*).

3. Performance criterion is specified (e.g., *on 8 of 10 consecutive times*).

    Note: The treatment objectives in the activities for Chapters 7-10 have the second component as listed above. Components 1 and 3 can be added for more specificity.

Pulling it all together

You are responsible for supplying wording for the IFSP that is in parent-friendly terms but also can be used to develop a treatment plan with measurable objectives. It can be challenging to interface these two types of documentation. Figure 12-3 demonstrates how to work from a broadly stated outcome supplied by the parent to selecting goals and treatment objectives and suggesting strategies and activities. A blank version of this form can be found in Appendix 12F, page 166. The form can also help you complete the *Priorities* section of the discipline-specific report. (See Appendix 12A, page 158.)

Selecting Goals, Treatment Objectives, Strategies, and Activities to Achieve Parent's Stated Outcome(s)

Outcome suggested by parent:	Parent wants Amanda to be able to tell the baby-sitter what she wants to drink and eat.		
In order to do this, you know that *Amanda* needs to:	**So you choose these goals and related treatment objectives:**	**You suggest these strategies:**	**You teach parents how to use the strategies in these activities:**
1. Understand the question the baby-sitter is asking	Receptive G4 Treatment objectives with activities R24, R27	Supplementing speech with gestures	At snack time, the baby-sitter will ask Amanda what she wants using speech and holding up the two objects from which to choose.
2. Use single words to answer questions	Expressive G5 Treatment objectives with activities E14, E18, E25, E28	Modeling the word; using gesture with the word	The baby-sitter will encourage Amanda to reach toward the object she wants and will model the word for Amanda and will encourage Amanda to imitate the word.
3. Produce consonants /j/ (*juice*), /w/ (*water*), /m/ (*milk*), /ch/ (*cheese*), and /k/ (*cookie*) for her favorite foods	Sound Production G3 Treatment objectives with activities S3, S6, S24, S33	Modeling the word; using touch cue with sound	The baby-sitter will say the word for each choice and use the touch cue for the initial sound.

Figure 12-3

Conversely, you must also be able to translate very specific treatment objectives into the strategies and activities for the parent to use. Figure 12-4 demonstrates how goals from a speech-language pathology treatment plan can be implemented by the parents/caregivers with specific strategies in activities at home. The form could also be used to select activities you will initiate in therapy. A blank form can be found in Appendix 12G, page 167.

Matching Goals and Objectives to Strategies and Activities for the Home

Goals for Sadie	Strategies	Activity during therapy	Activities for home
Expressive Goal 5: The child will increase spontaneous use of word combinations.	Setting up the environment	E47	1. When dressing Sadie, Dad will purposely hold up pants and say, "Here's your shirt" and prompt Sadie to say "not shirt." 2. When putting Sadie to bed, Mom will leave the light on, but say "light's out" and prompt Sadie to say "light not out."
Expressive Goal 5: The child will increase spontaneous use of word combinations.	Modeling and self-talk	E30, E34	1. When setting the table, Sadie's brother Sam will model the pronouns *my* and *your* by saying "my plate, your plate;" "my cup, your cup." 2. When taking a walk/ride in the wagon, Sadie's mom will get in the wagon and say "my turn to ride" and prompt Sadie to say "my turn."
Expressive Goal 5: The child will increase spontaneous use of word combinations.	Parallel talk and modeling	E27	1. When Sadie is playing with her toys, Mom or Dad will provide running description using verb + noun (e.g., "Drop ball," "Kiss baby," Feed baby"). 2. When giving Sadie a bath, Dad or Mom will describe each action with verb + noun (e.g., "Wash face," "Wash tummy").
Sound production Goal 3: The child will produce target consonants in words (final /t/).	Modeling	S34	1. Whenever Sadie wants to go outside, the adult with her should say, "You want to go out?" and stress the /t/. 2. Whenever it is time to eat, the adult with her should say "It's time to eat" and stress the /t/.
Sound production Goal 3: The child will produce target consonants in words (final /p/).	Physical prompt	S9	1. When Sadie wants to be put in the swing, the adult should say, "Let's get up" and help touch Sadie's lips together. 2. When Sadie wants a drink, the adult should say, "You'll need your cup" and stress the /p/ and help touch Sadie's lips together.
Sound production Goal 3: The child will produce target consonants in words (final /s/).	Modeling	S25	1. When Sadie's brother gets on the bus each morning, the adult should help Sadie say "bus" with the final /s/. 2. When Sadie is playing with her toy house, the adult should model the word *house* and help Sadie finish the word with an /s/.

Figure 12-4

It may be easier for the parents to work from a form that lists the activities of the day along with treatment objectives that can be addressed during that activity. A form like this might be completed every few weeks as new treatment objectives are selected. Figure 12-5 shows how this might be done. A blank version of this form can be found in Appendix 12H, page 168.

Matching Daily Activities to Treatment Objectives

Daily Activities	Skills/Treatment Objectives			
	Requests assistance from adult (P38)	Puts one object inside another (P40)	Identifies object by category (R25)	Asks for *more* (E26)
Waking up in crib in a.m.	Mom will wait in the door of the room when Sawyer wakes up so he will ask for help getting out of his crib.			
Eating breakfast	Mom will place food out of Sawyer's reach and wait for him to ask for help to reach the food.	While preparing food, Mom will place stacking cups on high chair tray.		Mom will pour a tiny bit of cereal in the bowl and then pause to see if Sawyer will ask for more.
Taking a bath			Mom will have toys in the tub in two different categories: animals and cups. She will ask Sawyer to "Find one we drink from" or "Find an animal."	Mom will tickle Sawyer with the washcloth and then pause and wait for him to ask for more.
Nap time		When taking off Sawyer's shoes and socks at nap time, Mom will encourage Sawyer to put his socks in his shoes.	Mom will reinforce the category name "clothes" by labeling each piece of clothing as "Let's take off your socks. Your socks are clothes."	
Dinner with family		While preparing dinner, Dad will provide bowls of different sizes so Sawyer can stack them.		
Story time	Sawyer's favorite book is placed out of reach but in sight. Parent will wait to see if Sawyer will ask for assistance to reach the book.			After reading a story, Dad will pause and then prompt Sawyer to ask for "more book" or "more read."

Figure 12-5

Chapter 12: Documentation

Using Progress Notes to Collect Data

Progress notes can be written in any form, but to ensure that all of the required information is included in each note, it is suggested that the S.O.A.P. format be used. The S.O.A.P. format uses four sections:

S (subjective)
This section contains subjective information about the child, including any statements made by the caregivers.

O (objective)
This section contains objective information about the child's performance during the session.

A (analysis)
This section contains the clinician's analysis and interpretation of how the session went. For example, did the child perform better on some tasks? Was the child more cooperative? Were there factors that interfered with the child's performance on this date?

P (plan)
This section notes what the clinician plans to do during the next session. It should also include what the family is to do before the next session.

In order to maximize your time, it is helpful to write as much of the progress note before and during the intervention session as possible. If the progress notes are structured to mirror the treatment objectives, the notes can be used to collect data on the child's performance during the session. (Note: This data can be put under the "O" section on the S.O.A.P. note, if that format is being used.) Some data (e.g., + and –, words the child says) must be collected on the note during the session.

When you first arrive at the child's home or day care, ask the caregiver about successes or challenges she has faced in addressing the treatment objectives since your last visit. Write these comments under the "S" section of the S.O.A.P. notes as the caregiver reports them to you.

As you wrap up the session, explain to the caregiver any specific strategies you want her to use during the following week. As you tell the caregiver the strategies, write them under the "P" section of the note. That way, when you exit the treatment session, you will only have to write the "A" section of the notes and perhaps add a few lines to the "O" section.

Figure 12-6 on the next page shows an example of a progress note indicating the sections that were filled out before the session, during the session, and the information that was added after the session. For a blank form that you can use, see Appendix 12I, page 169. (Note: The part of the note written in regular type was completed before the session, bold during the session, and script after the session.)

Chapter 12: Documentation

Speech and Language Progress Notes

Child's Name **Micaela**   Client # _____   Page _____

Date **August 21, 2004**

(Face-to-Face) or Phone	**S**: Micaela's mother stated that this week Micaela has pointed to her head, toes, and tummy while dressing. She has also asked "What's that?" at the grocery store.

Time In/Out **1300-1400**
 	
 Units: **4**
 	
 Code: _____
 	
 (Home/Community) or Office/Center
 	
 Family Involvement: Activities/ Strategies
	O: Receptive language treatment objectives:
	    Micaela will choose the object named by the SLP: **+ + + - + + + - - +**
	    Micaela will follow commands with: **push + + + + + +**
	                                                kiss - - + + + - +
	                                                drop + - - + +
	
	Expressive language treatment objectives:
	    Micaela will say 15 meaningful words: **mine, no, baby, da(that), uh oh, c'mon, ball, car**
	
	Micaela will ask "What's that?" **with objects hidden inside box.**
	Micaela asked "What's that?" with cues
	
	Sound production treatment objectives:
	    Micaela will use initial /d/ in imitation: **drop - - - + - +**
	                                              down + + - + +
	                                              Dad + + +

	A: *Micaela is doing much better choosing an object from a field of 5 and with no cues given. She wasn't as verbal today as during the last session, but "C'mon" was a new word for her! Her mother is doing a great job utilizing strategies taught.*
	P: Micaela's mom will encourage Micaela to say "push" with the toy boat in the bathtub. She will continue to hide things in a paper bag to encourage Micaela to ask "What's that?"

Figure 12-6

Six-Month Summary

The child's progress must be summarized every six months and shared with team members at an IFSP meeting. It is helpful, and in some instances required, to complete the six-month summary in the weeks before the meeting so that it can be shared with the parents and service coordinator before the meeting. A sample of a six-month progress report is provided in Appendix 12J, pages 170–171.

Sample Speech & Language Assessment

Appendix 12A

Name Serena B.   **Date of Assessment** 8-27-03

Birth Date 10-09-01   **Age** 23 months   **Adjusted Age** N/A

Parents Emory & Susan B.   **Referral Source** Initial Service Coordinator

Address _____   **Telephone** _____

Social Security # _____   **Case #** _____

Physician _____   **# Units** 4   **Time In/Out** 10:15/11:15

Primary Service Coordinator _____   **Setting** Child's home

Pertinent Medical History No significant medical history. Serena has had 4 ear infections, but has not had PE tubes. Serena was carried full-term with an uncomplicated birth.

Hearing Serena's hearing has not been tested since birth. No hearing loss was detected at that time.

State of Health Good though today she was a little stopped up.

Level of Response Serena was slow to warm up to the examiner, but after she did she participated well. This is typical per mother.

Persons Present Serena's mother (Susan) and the SLP

Sources/Measures Used

- ___ Behavioral checklist _____
- _X_ Standardized tests Zimmerman Preschool Language Scale
- _X_ Parent interview
- _X_ Criterion-referenced instrument The Rossetti Infant-Toddler Language Scale (see scores and comments attached.)
- _X_ Observation _____

Concerns Serena's mother is concerned that Serena is not using speech to communicate her wants and needs.

continued on next page

Therapy Guide
The Early Intervention Kit

Appendix 12A

Name Serena B.

Page 2

Priorities Susan would like Serena to be able to communicate with the other children when she attends Mother's Day Out program three mornings a week. She would also like to see a decrease in the screaming Serena exhibits when she can't make her needs known. She also wants Serena to be able to talk to her grandparents on the phone.

Strengths Serena has good receptive language skills. She uses gestures and pointing to communicate her wants and needs. She will sometimes imitate a word or sound. Susan is very eager to learn how to help Serena.

Needs Serena needs to improve her ability and willingness to imitate sounds and words, needs to use many more single words, and needs to begin using two-word combinations.

Emerging Skills Serena uses about 15 words per mother's report. The words are used infrequently and are not easily stimulated.

Materials and Equipment to Support Development Strategies include parent education of language stimulation techniques. The parent handout on strategies has been provided. In particular, Susan will begin to use parallel talk and self-talk, and will provide prompts to Serena. Serena would benefit from the addition of simple picture books in the home, with fewer pictures on a page.

Comments Serena uses approximately 15 words, per mother's report, on a regular basis. There are other words Serena has said, though not recently. The areas of gesture, play, and language comprehension are within age-appropriate limits. Pragmatics and expressive language are significantly delayed. Expressive skills are solid only through the 9-12 month level. There are no concerns about feeding/swallowing.

continued on next page

Appendix 12A

Name _Serena B._   Page _3_

Parent Education _The results of the assessment were shared verbally with Susan immediately following the assessment. Susan stated that she understood the results and agreed with the recommendations._

Diagnosis _Expressive Language Delay_

Eligibility _Child is eligible for Early Intervention services._

Rationale _Serena is eligible for services given the significance of her expressive language delay._

Recommend services be provided in natural environment? _Yes_

Recommendations _1. Refer for audiologic evaluation to rule out hearing loss._
2. Speech-language therapy to improve expressive language.

Signature of Speech-Language Pathologist   **Date**

Shared verbally with caregiver on _8-27-03_   (In Person)/Per Phone
Copy to caregiver given on _9-1-03_   (In Person)/Per Mail
Copy to Service Coordinator: Name _Doris Bell_   Date _9-1-03_   In Person/Mail/(Fax)
Copy to Pediatrician: Name _E. Cavell, M.D._   Date _9-1-03_   Mail/(Fax)

Age Performance Profile

Months	Interaction Attachment	Pragmatics	Gesture	Play	Language Comprehension	Language Expression	Months
33-36							33-36
30-33							30-33
27-30						1/6 17%	27-30
24-27			4/4 100%	2/3 67%	2/4 50%	0/5 0%	24-27
21-24			4/5 80%	3/3 100%	4/4 100%	0/8 0%	21-24
18-21		0/4 0%	5/5 100%			0/6 0%	18-21
15-18						2/7 29%	15-18
12-15						5/13 38%	12-15
9-12						8/8 100%	9-12
6-9							6-9
3-6							3-6
0-3							0-3

Therapy Guide
The Early Intervention Kit

Appendix 12B

Sample Speech-Language Pathology Treatment Plan and Discharge Summary

Services provided in _Home/Community_

Child's Name _Serena B._ **Birth Date** _10-09-01_ **Age** _23 months_ **Identification Number** _____

Primary Service Coordinator _____ **Date Therapy Initiated** _9-11-03_ **Terminated** _____

Total Units _____ **Diagnosis** _Expressive Language Delay_

Prognosis and Estimated Length of Treatment _good for age-appropriate skills; 9-12 months_

Long-term Goal _Serena will use expressive language typical of developmental peers._

Short-term Goals	Discharge Status
1. Serena will increase imitation of non-speech sounds, speech sounds, and sound sequences.	
a. Serena will imitate animal sounds.	
b. Serena will imitate other non-speech sounds.	
2. Serena will increase imitation of words.	
a. Serena will imitate the names of familiar objects.	
b. Serena will echo the last word of short phrases spoken during play.	
3. Serena will increase spontaneous use of single words to increase repertoire of communicative intents and communicative functions through activities such as _____.	
a. Serena will use exclamatory expressions (e.g. uh oh, no-no).	
b. Serena will ask for more of an object or an activity.	
c. Serena will name pictures in books to label objects.	
d. Serena will use her own name to answer questions.	
e. Serena will name body parts on herself and others	
f. Serena will use early developing modifiers (e.g., big, hot).	

Summary Statement _____

_____

Follow-up _____

_____

_____   _____
Signature of Speech-Language Pathologist   Date

Shared verbally with caregiver on _8-27-03_   (In Person)/Per Phone
Copy to caregiver given on _9-6-03_   (In Person)/Per Mail
Copy to Service Coordinator: Name _Merlinda Lockspur_   Date _9-4-03_   In Person/(Mail)/Fax
Copy to Pediatrician: Name _E. Cavell, M.D._   Date _9-4-03_   (Mail)/Fax

Therapy Guide
The Early Intervention Kit   Copyright © 2004 LinguiSystems, Inc.

Appendix 12C

Sample Individualized Family Service Plan (IFSP)
Family Resources, Concerns, and Priorities

Child's Name _Serena B._   Birth Date _10-9-00_   Today's Date _9-6-03_

Concerns: What concerns do you have regarding your child's development? _Serena's mom (Susan) is concerned with Serena's speech. She uses fewer than 20 words. She is having a little difficulty with her gross motor skills. She is clumsy and falls a lot._

Priorities: How can our services address your concerns without disrupting your family routines/schedule? _Serena will receive therapy at home on the days she is not attending Mother's Day out program._

Resources: What helps you care for your child? _Serena is motivated by books, puzzles, and crayons. Her extended family is very involved in her care. She attends Mother's Day Out three mornings a week._

Present Level of Functioning	Information provided by:
Vision/Hearing/Health Immunizations _Serena's vision is good and her immunizations are up to date. A hearing test is pending to rule out hearing loss._	Susan, Nancy (SLP)
Personal—Social Development (Getting along with others) _Serena is very social. There are no concerns in this area._	Susan, Isobel (PT)
Adaptive Development (Doing things for him/herself) _Serena is doing well. There are no concerns in this area._	Susan, Isobel (PT)
Motor Development (Movement) _She throws a ball and kicks it. She has a neat pencil grasp, colors, and walks._	Isobel (PT)
Communication Development (Understanding and expression) _Serena has very good comprehension. She is adding new words._	Nancy (SLP), Susan
Cognitive Development (Thinking and learning) _Serena is doing well in this area._	Nancy (SLP), Isobel (PT)

continued on next page

Therapy Guide
The Early Intervention Kit

Appendix 12C

Outcome #	Date Initiated	Child/Family Outcomes (statement of change for family or child)	Strategies/Activities (Practical Suggestions to meet outcomes)	Responsible Parties/Services (who, frequency, intensity)	Setting/ Location	Review and progress (dates achieved, family comments and initials)
1	9-6-03	Serena will use more words to communicate her wants and needs.	1. During daily activities (e.g., bath time, riding in the car, dinner), parents will use self-talk and parallel talk to model one-word and two-word utterances for Serena. 2. During bath time and when dressing Serena, parents will ask Serena to imitate names of body parts. 3. When playing outside with Serena, parents will ask her to imitate environmental sounds they hear (e.g., sirens, birds, dogs). 4. When reading books, parents will point to objects and actions and model one-word utterances for Serena to imitate. 5. Parents will put favorite items out of Serena's reach to encourage her to use words to request them. 6. When Serena points or screams to get an item, parents will provide a choice of two words (e.g., Do you want juice or milk?) and wait for Serena to respond.	Nancy (SLP) will visit Serena's home 1X week for one hour; parents will implement strategies on daily basis.	Child's home 1X week; Mother will try to arrange to have same-age cousin present for one session a month to serve as a model.	

continued on next page

Therapy Guide
The Early Intervention Kit

Appendix 12C

Outcome #	Date Initiated	Child/Family Outcomes (statement of change for family or child)	Strategies/Activities (Practical Suggestions to meet outcomes)	Responsible Parties/Services (who, frequency, intensity)	Setting/ Location	Review and progress (dates achieved, family comments and initials)
2	9-6-03	Serena will independently climb up and down stairs so she can be more independent in the home and community.	1. Serena's parents will hold Serena's hand and place her other hand on the banister when they climb the stairs at home. 2. Serena's parents will put Serena on the third step from the bottom and place her hand on the banister and encourage her to finish the last three steps on her own.	Isabel (PT) will see Serena 2X month in her home for 2 months, and then decrease visits to monthly. Parents to practice daily.	PT services will be provided in the home.	
3	9-6-03	Serena will be independent with balance skills so that she will have increased safety and confidence in her daily activities.	1. Serena's parents will hold her hands and help her practice tip-toe walking when going down the hall from bedroom to bathroom. 2. Serena's parents will take Serena on walks outside and hold her hand as she walks along short brick wall around the park.			
4	9-6-03	Serena's family will receive service planning and coordination in order to access services in a timely manner that will promote her development.	1. Melinda will contact the family at least once a month to check on satisfaction with services. 2. Melinda will be available on a regular basis to answer questions and assist with any needs that might arise. 3. Coordinate a review of Serena's progress every six months or sooner if needed.	Melinda (PSC) at least one contact per month at home or by phone.	Melinda in child's home and in office (by phone).	

Therapy Guide
The Early Intervention Kit

Appendix 12D

Speech and Language Progress Notes
(IFSP Meetings)

Child's Name _____ Case # _____ Page _____

Date _____

Face-to-Face or Phone Time In/Out Units _____ Code _____ Home/Community or Office/Center	Use of private insurance was/was not discussed during the IFSP meeting. Family chose to use/not use insurance. Name of insurance company _____ Copy of card obtained yes/no Provision of services in natural environment was/was not discussed during the meeting. Services will be provided in a natural environment. yes/no Some services will be provided in a natural environment (Specify) _____ _____ _____ _____ Plans to transition to natural environment _____ _____ _____ _____ _____ _____ _____ _____

Discipline: SLP   Signature _____

Appendix 12E

Developing Outcomes from Daily Activities

Time	Activity	What the child does	What the caregiver does	Potential child outcome/goal	Potential family member strategy

Appendix 12F

Selecting Goals, Treatment Objectives, Strategies, and Activities to Achieve Parent's Stated Outcome(s)

Outcome suggested by parent _____

_____

In order to do this, you know that _____ needs to:	So you choose these goals and related treatment objectives:	You suggest these strategies:	You teach parents how to use the strategies in these activities:

Appendix 12G

Matching Goals and Objectives to Strategies and Activities for the Home

Goals for _____	Strategies	Activity during therapy	Activities for home
			1. 2.
			1. 2.
			1. 2.
			1. 2.
			1. 2.
			1. 2.
			1. 2.

Appendix 12H

Matching Daily Activities to Treatment Objectives

Daily Activities	Skills/Treatment Objectives			

Appendix 12I

Speech and Language Progress Notes

Child's Name _____ Case # _____ Page _____

Date _____

Face-to-Face or Phone	
Time In/Out	
Units _____	
Code _____	
Home/Community or Office/Center	
Family Involvement: Activities/ Strategies	

Discipline: SLP   Signature _____

Sample Six-Month Progress Report

Appendix 12J

Name Serena B.   **Case #** _____

Service Site _____   **Service** _____   **Name of PSC** _____

Birth Date 10-09-01   **Age** 28 months   **Frequency and Intensity** 1X/week for 4 units

Child's actual attendance (number out of total possible contacts) _____

Six-Month Progress Serena has been seen once a week for an hour to target expressive language skills. Currently, Serena has met all goals established at the time of assessment. She has just begun using two-word utterances consistently like "batteries work" and "bye-bye boat." Serena continues to exhibit a mild expressive language delay with mastery at the 21-24 month level per the Rossetti Infant-Toddler Language Scale. She demonstrates emerging skills up to the 33-36 month level as she is using such language as negation (e.g., "don't") and prepositions (e.g., "on, in, off", and "out"). Therapy continues without concerns in the areas of receptive language, play, gesture, pragmatics, and interaction/attachment as Serena demonstrates skills appropriate not only at her age level, but many skills beyond her age level. Therapy also informally targeted articulation skills such as final /p/ and final /t/ which Serena mastered.

Services provided in natural environment? yes

Recommendations Continue speech therapy once a week to target expressive language skills and monitor articulation skills.

Strategies/Activities 1. Serena's family will expand her utterances by repeating her utterances and adding a word (e.g., Serena says "juice please" and Mother responds with "more juice please"). The family will do this while playing with Serena and at opportunities throughout the day when Serena is requesting items.

2. Serena's family will read and speak slowly to Serena to emphasize speech sounds.

continued on next page

Appendix 12J

Name Serena B. Page 2

3. Serena's parents will decrease use of questions that can be answered with yes/no and ask questions that require longer responses (e.g., "Where are some places bear could hide?" "What do you like to do?").

4. Serena's parents will use sabotage to elicit more spontaneous utterances (e.g., at bath time they'll purposely hide Serena's favorite bath toy and wait for her to ask for it).

Date 2-19-03   **Signature/Title of Person Completing Report** _____

Shared verbally with caregiver on 2-12-03   (In Person)/Per Phone
Copy to caregiver given on 2-21-03   (In Person)/Per Mail
Copy to Service Coordinator: Name _____ Date 2-21-03   In Person/(Mail)/Fax
Copy to Pediatrician: Name E. Cavell, M.D.   Date 2-21-03   (Mail)/Fax

References

Abraham, S. (2003). Babies with Tracheostomies: The challenge of providing specialized clinical care. *The ASHA Leader, 8,* 4-5.

Affleck, G., Tennen, H., Rowe, J., Roscher, B., & Walker, L. (1989). Effects of former support on mothers' adaptation to the hospital-to-home transition of high-risk infants: The benefits and costs of helping. *Child Development, 60,* 488-501.

Ainsworth, M., Blehar, M., Walters, E., & Wall, S. (1978). *Patterns of attachments: A psychological study of the strange situation.* Hillsdale, NJ: Lawrence Erlbaum Associates.

Als, H. (1997). Earliest intervention for preterm infants in the newborn intensive care units. In M. J. Guralnick (Ed.), *The effectiveness of early intervention.* Baltimore: Paul H. Brookes Publishing Co.

American Speech-Language-Hearing Association. (1990). The roles of speech-language pathologists in service delivery to infants, toddlers and their families. *Asha, 32* (Suppl. 2), 4.

American Speech-Language-Hearing Association. (1991). Report: Augmentative and alternative communication. *Asha, 33* (Suppl. 5), 9-12.

Anderson, N. B. & McNeilly, L. G. (1992). Meeting the needs of special populations. In M. Bender & C. A. Baglin (Eds.), *Infants and toddlers: A resource guide for practitioners.* San Diego: Singular Publishing Group.

Antoniadis, A., Didow, S., Lockhart, S., & Morogue, P. (1984). Adapted from Screening for early cognitive and communicative behaviors. *Communique, 9,* 14.

Apel, K. & Masterson, J. J. (2001). *Beyond baby talk: From sounds to sentences—A parent's complete guide to language development.* Roseville, CA: Prima Publishing.

Apfel, N. H. (2001). The birth of a new instrument: The infant-toddler and family instrument (ITFI). *Zero to Three, 21,* 4, 29-35.

Attwood, T. (1998). *Asperger's syndrome: A guide for parents and professionals.* London, England: Jessica Kingsley Publishers.

Baer, D. (1981). The nature of intervention research. In R. Schiefelbusch & D. Bricker (Eds.), *Early language: Acquisition and intervention* (pp. 559-573). Baltimore: University Park Press.

Bailey, D. B., McWilliam, R. A., Darkes, L. A., Hebbeler, K., Simeonsson, R. J., Spiker, D., & Wagner, M. (1998). Family outcomes in early intervention: A framework for program evaluation and efficacy research. *Exceptional Children: Journal of the International Council for Exceptional Children, 64,* 3, 313-28.

Bailey, D. B. & Wolder, M. R. (1984). *Teaching infants and preschoolers with handicaps.* Columbus, OH: Charles E. Merrill.

Bailey, E. & Bricker, D. (1985). Evaluation of a three-year early-intervention demonstration project. *Topics in Early Childhood Special Education, 5,* 2, 52-65.

Ballinger, R. (1999). YAACK: Augmentative communication resource guide for young kids. http://home.hawaii.rr.com/wenlu/yaack/index.html

Bashir, A., Grahamjones, F., & Bostwick, R. (1984). A touch-cue method of therapy for developmental verbal apraxia. *Seminars in Speech and Language, 5,* 2, 127-137.

Bates, E., Bretherton, I., & Snyder, L. (1988). *From first words to grammar: Individual differences and dissociable mechanisms.* New York: Cambridge University Press.

Bellugi, U. & Brown, R. (Eds.). (1964). The acquisition of language. *Monographs of the Society for Research in Child Development, 29*, (serial no. 92).

Bender, M. & Baglin, C. A. (1992). *Infants and toddlers: A resource guide for practitioners*. San Diego, CA: Singular Publishing Group, Inc.

Bennett, F. C. (1995). Recent advances in developmental intervention for biologically vulnerable infants. In J. A. Blackman (Ed.), *Treatment options in early intervention*. Gaithersburg MD: Aspen Publishers.

Bernthal, J. E. & Bankson, N. W. (1981). *Articulation disorders*. Englewood Cliffs, NJ: Prentice-Hall, Inc.

Beukelman, D. R., & Ansel, B. (1995). Research priorities in augmentative and alternative communication. *Augmentative and Alternative Communication, 11*, 131-134.

Beukelman, D. R., & Mirenda, P. (1998). *Augmentative and alternative communication: Management of severe communication disorders in children and adults* (2nd ed.). Baltimore: Paul H. Brookes Publishing Co.

Blackman, J. (Ed.). (1995) *Treatment options in early intervention*. Gaithersburg, MD: Aspen Publishers.

Blakely, R. (1983). Treatment of developmental apraxia of speech. In W. Perkins (Ed.), *Dysarthria and apraxia*. New York: Thieme-Stratton Corp.

Bloom, L. (1973). *One word at a time: The use of single-word utterances before syntax*. The Hague: Mouton.

Bloom, L. & Lahey, M. (1978). *Language development and language disorders*. New York: John Wiley & Sons.

Bloomberg, K., Karlan, G. R., & Lloyd, L. L. (1990). The comparative translucency of initial lexical items represented in five graphic symbol systems and sets. *Journal of Speech and Hearing Research, 33*, 717-725.

Bluma, A., Shearer, M., Frohman, A., & Hillard, J. (1976). *Portage guide to early education*. Portage, WI: The Portage Project, CESA 12.

Bodine, C. & Beukelman, D. R. (1991). Prediction of future speech performance among potential users of AAC systems: A survey. *Augmentative and Alternative Communication, 7*, 112-116.

Bond, L., Creasy, G., & Abrams, C. (1990). Play assessment: Reflecting and promoting cognitive competence. In E. Gibbs & D. Teti (Eds.), *Interdisciplinary assessment of infants: A guide for early intervention professionals* (p. 382). Baltimore: Paul H. Brookes Publishing Co.

Bondy, A. S., & Frost, L. A. (1993). Mands across the water: A report on the application of the picture-exchange communication system in Peru. *The Behavior Analyst, 16*, 123-128.

Bornstein, H., Saulnier, K. L., & Hamilton, L. B. (1983). *The comprehensive signed English dictionary*. Washington, DC: Gallaudet University Press.

Bricker, D., Bruder, M., & Bailey, E. (1982). Developmental integration of preschool children. *Analysis and Intervention in Developmental Disabilities, 2*, 207-222.

Bricker, D. & Cripe, J. J. (1992). *An activity-based approach to early intervention*. Baltimore: Paul H. Brookes Publishing Co.

Bricker, D. & Gumerlock, S. (1988). Application of a three-level evaluation plan for monitoring child progress and program effects. *Journal of Special Education, 22*, 1, 66-81.

Bricker, D. & Sheehan, R. (1981). Effectiveness of an early intervention program as indexed by child change. *Journal of the Division for Early Childhood. 4*, 11-27.

Brown, R. (1973). *A first language, the early stages.* Cambridge, MA: Harvard University Press.

Bruner, J. (1975). The ontogenesis of speech acts. *Journal of Child Language, 2*, 1-19.

Bruner, J. (1977). Early social interaction and language acquisition. In H. Schaffer (Ed.), *Studies in mother-infant interaction* (pp. 271-289). New York: Academic Press.

Bryant, D. & Ramey, C. (1987). An analysis of the effectiveness of early intervention programs for environmentally at-risk children. In M. Guralnick and F. Bennett (Eds.), *The effectiveness of early intervention for at-risk and handicapped children* (p. 58). Orlando: Academic Press.

Chang, H. N. & Pulido, D. (1994). The critical importance of cultural and linguistic continuity for infants and toddlers. *Zero to Three, 15*, 2, 13-17.

Chapman, K. L. & Terrell, B. Y. (1994). "Verb-alizing": Facilitating action word usage in young language-impaired children. In K. G. Butler (Ed.), *Early intervention I: Working with infants and toddlers.* Gaithersburg, MD: Aspen Publishers.

Chapman, R. (1981). Adapted from Exploring children's communicative intents. In J. Miller's *Assessing language production in children: Experimental procedures.* Boston: Allyn & Bacon.

Chapman, R. & Miller, J. (1975). Word order in early two and three word utterances: Does production precede comprehension? *Journal of Speech and Hearing Research, 18*, 2, 355-371.

Clark, C. R. (1981). Learning words using traditional orthography and the symbols of Rebus, Bliss, and Carrier. *Journal of Speech and Hearing Disorders, 46*, 191-196.

Coggins, T. E. & Carpenter, R. L. (1981). The communication intention inventory: A system for observing and coding children's early intentional communication. *Applied Psycholinguistics, 2*, 235-251.

Cole, K., Dale, P., & Mills, P. (1991). Individual differences in language delayed children's responses to direct and interactive preschool instruction. *Topics in Early Childhood Special Education, 11*, 1, 99-124.

Coleman, J. G. (1993). *The early intervention dictionary.* Bethesda, MD: Woodbine House.

Coleman, P. P., Buysse, V., Scalise-Smith, D. L. & Schulte, A. C. (1995). Consultation: Applications to early intervention. In J. Blackman (Ed.), *Treatment options in early intervention.* Gaithersburg, MD: Aspen Publishers.

Costello, E. (1983). *Signing: How to speak with your hands.* New York: Bantam Books.

Cunningham, C. & Sloper, P. (1980). *Helping your exceptional baby.* New York: Pantheon Books.

Dale, P. S. (1991). The validity of a parent report measure of vocabulary and syntax at 24 months. *Journal of Speech and Hearing Research, 34*, 656-571.

Dale, P. S., Bates, E., Reznick, S., & Morisset, C. (1989). The validity of a parent report instrument of child language at 20 months. *Journal of Child Language, 16*, 239-250.

Dawson, G. & Osterling, J. (1997). Early intervention in autism. In M. J. Guralnick (Ed.), *The effectiveness of early intervention* (pp. 307-326). Baltimore: Paul H. Brookes Publishing Co.

de Villiers, J. & de Villiers, P. (1973). Development of the use of word order in comprehension. *Journal of Psycholinguistic Research, 2,* 331-341.

Dewey, J. (1959). *Dewey on education.* New York: Columbia University, Bureau of Publications.

Dore, J. (1975). Holophrases, speech acts, and language universals. *Journal of Child Language, 2,* 21-40.

Dunham, J. K. (1989). The transparency of manual signs in a linguistic and an environmental nonlinguistic context. *Augmentative and Alternative Communication, 5,* 214-225.

Dunst, C. J. (1981). *Infant learning.* Allen, TX: DLM Teaching Resources.

Dyson, A. & Paden, E. (1983). Some phonological acquisition strategies used by two-year olds. *Journal of Childhood Communication Disorders, 7,* 6-18.

Erikson, J. (2001). From demonstration model into the real world: Some experiences with IDA. *Zero to Three, 21,* 4, 20-28.

Ervin-Tripp, S. (1970). Discourse agreement: How children answer questions. In J. Hayes (Ed.), *Language acquisition models and methods.* New York: Academic Press.

Feldman, M. A., Sparks, B., & Case, L. (1993). Effectiveness of home-based early intervention on the language development of children of mothers with mental retardation. *Research in Developmental Disabilities, 14,* 5, 387-408.

Fenson, L., Dale, P., Reznick, J., Thal, D., Bates, E., Hartung, J., Pethick, S., & Reilly, J. (1993). *MacArthur communicative development inventories: User's guide and technical manual.* San Diego: Singular Publishing Group.

Filler, J. (1983). Service models for handicapped infants. In S. Gray Garwood & R. Fewell (Eds.), *Educating handicapped infants* (p. 290). Rockville, MD: Aspen Publishers.

Fuller, D. R., & Lloyd, L. L. (1991). Forum: Toward a common usage of iconicity terminology. *Augmentative and Alternative Communication, 7,* 215-220.

Furuno, S., O'Reilly, K. A., Hosake, C. M., Inatsuka, T. T., Allman, T. L., & Ziesloft, B. (1979). *Hawaii early learning profile.* Palo Alto, CA: VORT Corporation.

Gerber, S. E. (1998). *Etiology and prevention of communicative disorders,* (2nd ed.). San Diego, CA: Singular Publishing Group, Inc.

Gilbert, M. A., Sciarillo, W. G., & Von Rembow, D. L. (1992). Service coordination through case management. In M. Bender & C. A. Baglin (Eds.), *Infants and toddlers: A resource guide for practitioners.* San Diego: Singular Publishing Group.

Girolametto, L. (1988). Improving the social-conversational skills of developmentally delayed children: An intervention study. *Journal of Speech Hearing Disorders, 53,* 156.

Giumento, A. (1990). *The effectiveness of two intervention procedures on the acquisition and generalization of object labels by young children who are at risk or who have developmental delays.* Unpublished doctoral dissertation, University of Oregon. Eugene.

Glennen, S. L. & DeCoste, D. C. (1997). *The handbook of augmentative and alternative communication.* San Diego: Singular Publishing Group.

Grantham-McGregor, S. (1987). Development of severely malnourished children who received psychosocial stimulation: Six year follow-up. *Pediatrics, 79*, 48.

Grunwell, P. (1987). *Clinical phonology* (2nd ed.). Baltimore: Williams & Wilkins.

Guitar, B. (1998). *Stuttering: An integrated approach to its nature and treatment* (2nd ed.). Baltimore: Lippincott Williams & Wilkins.

Guralnick, M. J. (1993). Second generation research on effectiveness of early intervention. *Early Education and Development, 4*, 368.

Guralnick, M. J. (Ed.). (1997). *The effectiveness of early intervention.* Baltimore: Paul H. Brookes Publishing Co.

Hall, D. (1999). Letter to the editor. *International Journal of Language and Communication Disorders, 34*, 4, 445-447.

Haney, M. & Klein, M. D. (1993). Impact of a program to facilitate mother-infant communication in high-risk families of high-risk infants. *Journal of Childhood Communication Disorders, 5*, 1, 15-22.

Hanft, B. E. & Pilkington, K. O. (2000). Therapy in natural environments: The means or end goal for early intervention? *Infants and Young Children, 12*, 4, 1.

Hanft, B. & Von Rembow, D. L. (1992). The individualized family service plan process. In M. Bender & C. A. Baglin (Eds.), *Infants and toddlers: A resource guide for practitioners.* San Diego: Singular Publishing Group, Inc.

Hanson, M. J. (1977). *Teaching your Down's syndrome infant.* Baltimore: University Park Press.

Hardy, J. (1984). Cleft lip and palate. In J. Blackman (Ed.), *Medical aspects of developmental disabilities in children birth to three.* Rockville, MD: Aspen Publishers.

Hare, G. (1983). Development at 2 years. In J. V. Irwin & S. P. Wong (Eds.), *Phonological development in children: 18-72 months.* Carbondale, IL: Southern Illinois University Press.

Hart, B. & Risley, T. R. (1974). Using preschool materials to modify the language of disadvantaged children. *Journal of Applied Behavioral Analysis, 7*, 243-256.

Healy, A. (1984). Cerebral palsy. In J. Blackman (Ed.), *Medical aspects of developmental disabilities in children birth to three.* Rockville, MD: Aspen Publishers.

Hedrick, D. L., Prather, E. M., & Tobin, A. R. (1975). *Sequenced inventory of communication development.* Seattle: University of Washington Press.

Heincke, C., Beckwith, L., & Thompson, A. (1989). Early intervention in the family system: A framework and review. *Infant Mental Health Journal, 9*, 2.

Heriza, C. B. & Sweeney, J. K. (1990). Effects of NICU intervention on preterm infants: Part 1. Implications for neonatal practice. *Infants and Young Children, 2*, 3, 31-47.

Hershberger, P. (1991). A naturalistic approach to home-based early intervention. *The Transdisciplinary Journal 1*, 2, 83.

Hodson, B. W. & Paden, E. (1983). *Targeting intelligible speech: A phonological approach to remediation.* San Diego: College Hill Press.

Hoge, D. R. & Newsome, C. A. (2001). *The source for augmentative alternative communication.* East Moline, IL: LinguiSystems, Inc.

Holland, A. (1975). Language therapy for children: Some thoughts on context and content. *Journal of Speech and Hearing Disorders, 40,* 183-199.

Ingram, D. (1976). *Phonological disability in children.* London: Arnold.

Ireton, H. & Thwing, E. (1974). *The Minnesota child development inventory.* Minneapolis: University of Minnesota.

Jacobsen, C., Starnes, C., & Gasser, V. (1988). An experimental analysis of the generalization of description and praises for mothers of premature infants. *Human Communication, 12,* 23.

Johnson-Martin, N. M., Jens, K. G., Attermeier, S. M., & Hacker, B. J. (1991). *The Carolina curriculum for infants and toddlers with special needs.* Baltimore: Paul H. Brookes Publishing Co.

Jung, J. H. (1989). *Genetic syndromes in communication disorders.* Austin, TX: Pro-Ed.

Kaiser, A., Hendrickson, J., & Alpert, C. (1991). Milieu language teaching: A second look. In R. Gable (Ed.), *Advances in mental retardation and developmental disabilities,* Vol. IV, (pp. 63-92). London: Jessica Kingsley Publisher.

Khan, L. & Lewis, N. (1986). *Khan-Lewis phonological analysis.* Circle Pines, MN: American Guidance Service.

Klaus, M. & Kennell, J. (1976). *Maternal-infant bonding.* St. Louis: C.V. Mosby.

Korsten, J. E., Dunn, D. K., Foss, T. V., & Francke, M. K. (1993). *Every move counts: Sensory-based communication techniques.* Overland Park, KS: Responsive Management, Inc.

Lahey, M. (1988). *Language disorders and language development.* New York, Macmillan.

Lahey, M. & Bloom. L. (1977). Planning a first lexicon: Which words to teach first. *Journal of Speech and Hearing Disorders, 42,* 340-349.

LeLaurin, K. (1992). Infant and toddler models of service delivery: Are they detrimental for some children and families? *Topics in Early Childhood Special Education, 12,* 1, 82.

Letts, C. & Edwards, S. (1999). Letter to the editor. *International Journal of Language and Communication Disorders, 34,* 4, 443-445.

Light, J. C. & Binger, C. (1998). *Building communicative competence with individuals who use augmentative and alternative communication.* Baltimore: Paul H. Brookes Publishing Co.

Linder, T. W. (1990). *Transdisciplinary play-based assessment: A functional approach to working with young children.* Baltimore: Paul H. Brookes Publishing Co.

Lloyd, L. L., Fuller, D. R., & Arvidson, H. H. (1997). *Augmentative and alternative communication: A handbook of principles and practices.* Boston: Allyn and Bacon.

Losardo, A. & Bricker, D. (1994). Activity-based intervention and direct instruction: A comparison study. *American Journal on Mental Retardation, 98,* 6, 774.

Lund, N. J. & Duchan, J. F. (1988). *Assessing children's language in naturalistic contexts.* Englewood Cliffs, NJ: Prentice-Hall, Inc.

MacDonald, J. (1989). *Becoming partners with children: From play to conversation*. San Antonio, TX: Special Press.

MacDonald, J. D. & Carroll, J. Y. (1995). A partnership model for communicating with infants at risk. In J. A. Blackman (Ed.), *Treatment options in early intervention*. Gaithersburg, MD: Aspen Publishers.

Mahoney, G. & Powell, A. (1988). Modifying parent-child interaction: Enhancing the development of handicapped children. *Journal of Special Education, 22*, 1, 82-96.

Marschark, M. (1993). *Psychological development of deaf children*. New York: Oxford University Press.

McCarthy, J. (1980). Assessment of young children with learning problems: Beyond the paralysis of analysis. In E. Sell (Ed.), *Follow-up of the high-risk newborn: A practical approach* (p. 59). Springfield, IL: Charles C. Thomas.

McCormick, L. & Schiefelbusch, R. L. (Eds.). (1990). *Early language intervention: An introduction* (2nd ed.). Columbus, OH: Merrill.

McCune-Nicolich, L. (1981). The cognitive bases of relational words in the single word period. *Journal of Child Language, 8*, 15-34.

McDonnell, A. & Hardman, M. (1988). A synthesis of "best practice" guidelines for early childhood services. *Journal of the Division for Early Childhood, 12*, 328-341.

McEwen, I. R. & Lloyd, L. L. (1990). Some considerations about the motor requirements of manual signs. *Augmentative and Alternative Communication, 6*, 207-216.

McLean, J. E. & Snyder-McLean, L. K. (1978). *A transactional approach to early language training*. Columbus, OH: Bell & Howell Company.

McLean, L. K. & Cripe, J. W. (1997). The effectiveness of early intervention for children with communication disorders. In M. J. Guralnick (Ed.), *The effectiveness of early intervention*. Baltimore: Paul H. Brookes Publishing Co.

McNaughron, D. (1994). Measuring parent satisfaction with early childhood intervention programs: Current practice, problems, and future perspectives. *Topics in Early Childhood Special Education, 14*, 26-48.

McWilliam, R. A. (1996). A program of research on integrated versus isolated treatment in early intervention. In R. A. McWilliam (Ed.), *Rethinking pull-out services in early intervention* (pp. 71-102). Baltimore: Paul H. Brookes Publishing Co.

McWilliam, R. A., Lang, L., Vandiviere, P., Angell, R., Collins, L., & Underdown, G. (1995a). Satisfaction and struggles: Family perceptions of early intervention services. *Journal of Early Intervention, 19*, 43-60.

McWilliam, R. A., Tocci, L., & Harbin, G. (1995b). *Services are child-oriented, and families like it that way-But why?* Early Childhood Research Institute on Service Utilization, Frank Potter Graham Child Development Center, University of North Carolina at Chapel Hill.

Meisels, S. J. & Provence, S. (1989). *Screening and assessment: Guidelines for identifying young disabled and developmentally vulnerable children and their families*. National Center for Clinical Infant Programs, Washington, D.C.

Miller, J. (1981). *Assessing language production in children: Experimental procedures*. Boston: Allyn and Bacon.

Miller, K. (1990). *More things to do with toddlers and twos*. West Palm Beach, FL: Telshare Publishing Co., Inc.

Miller, K. (2000). *Things to do with toddlers and twos*. West Palm Beach, FL: Telshare Publishing Co., Inc.

Mirenda, P. & Locke, P. A. (1989). A comparison of symbol transparency in nonspeaking persons with intellectual disabilities. *Journal of Speech and Hearing Disorders, 54*, 131-140.

Mirenda, P. & Mathy-Laikko, P. (1989). Augmentative and alternative communication applications for persons with severe congenital communication disorders: An introduction. *Augmentative and Alternative Communication, 5*, 3-13.

Mizuko, M. (1987). Transparency and ease of learning of symbols represented by Blissymbols, PCS, and Picsyms. *Augmentative and Alternative Communication, 3*, 129-136.

Moeller, M. P. (2000). Early intervention and language development in children who are deaf and hard of hearing. *Pediatrics, 106*, E43.

Murphy, T., Nichter, C., & Liden, C. (1982). Developmental outcome of the high-risk infant: A review of methodological issues. *Seminars in Perinatology, 6*, 4.

Nelson, K. (1973). Structure and strategy in learning to talk. *Monographs of the Society for Research in Child Development, 38*, (serial no. 149).

Nelson, K. (1986). Event knowledge and cognitive. In K. Nelson (Ed.), *Event knowledge: Structure and function in development* (pp 1-18). Hillsdale NJ: Erlbaum.

Noonan, M. J. & McCormick, L. (1993). *Early intervention in natural environments: Methods & procedures.* Albany: Delmar Learning.

Northcott, W. H. (1977). *Curriculum guide: Hearing-impaired children, birth to three years, and their parents.* Washington, D.C: Alexander Graham Bell Association for the Deaf.

Ogletree, B. T. & Daniels, D. B. (1995). Communication-based assessment and intervention for pre-linguistic infants and toddlers: Strategies and issues. In J. Blackman (Ed.), *Identification and assessment in early intervention.* Gaithersburg, MD: Aspen Publishers.

O'Hanlon, L. & Thal, D. (1991). *MacArthur CDI/Toddlers: Validation for language impaired children.* Paper presented at the convention of the American Speech-Language-Hearing Association, Atlanta, GA.

Olson, H. C. & Burgess, D. M. (1997). Early intervention for children prenatally exposed to alcohol and other drugs. In M. J. Guralnick (Ed.), *The effectiveness of early intervention.* Baltimore: Paul H. Brookes Publishing Co.

Orlansky, M. D., & Bonvillian, J. D. (1984). The role of iconicity in early sign language acquisition. *Journal of Speech and Hearing Disorders, 49*, 287-292.

O'Rourke, T. (Ed.). (1973). *A basic course in manual communication.* Silver Spring, MD: The National Association of the Deaf.

Owens, R. (1992). *Language development: An introduction* (3rd ed.). New York: Macmillan Publishing Company.

Owens, R. E. (1996). *Language development: An introduction* (4th ed.). Boston: Allyn and Bacon.

Padden, C. & Humphries, T. (1988). Deaf in America: Voices from a culture. Cambridge, MA: Harvard University Press. In M. J. Guralnick (Ed.), *The effectiveness of early intervention.* Baltimore: Paul H. Brookes Publishing Co.

Paul, R. (1995). *Language disorders from infancy through adolescence: Assessment & intervention.* St. Louis: Mosby-Year Book, Inc.

Pendergast, K., Dickey, S., Selmar, J., and Soder, A. (1969). *Photo articulation test*. Danville, IL: Interstate Printers and Publishers.

Perkins, W. H. (Ed.) (1983). *Dysarthria and apraxia*. NYC: Thieme-Stratton, Inc.

Piaget, J. (1926). *Language and thought of the child*. London: Routledge & Kegan Paul.

Piaget, J. (1970). Piaget's theory. In P. Mussen (Ed.), *Carmichael's manual of child psychology*, (Vol. 1). New York: John Wiley & Sons.

Prather, E., Hedrick, D., & Kern, D. (1975). Articulation development in children aged two to four years. *Journal of Speech and Hearing Disorders, 40*, 179-191.

Pressman, L. J. (1998). A comparison of the links between emotional availability and language gain in young children with and without hearing loss. *Volta Review, 100*, 5, 251.

Prizant, B. M. & Wetherby, A. M. (1995). Communication and language assessment for young children. In J. Blackman (Ed.), *Identification and assessment in early intervention*. Gaithersburg, MD: Aspen Publishers.

Prizant, B., Wetherby, A., & Roberts, J. (2000). Adapted from Communication disorders in infants and toddlers. In C. Zeanah (Ed.), *Handbook of infant mental health*. New York: Guilford Press.

Reznick, J. S. & Goldfield, L. (1989). A multiple word production checklist for assessing early language. *Journal of Child Language, 16*, 91-100.

Richard, G. J. & Hoge, D. R. (1999). *The source for syndromes*. East Moline, IL: LinguiSystems, Inc.

Riekehof, L. L. (1987). The joy of signing (2nd ed.). Springfield, MO: Gospel Publishing House.

Rivers, K. & Hendrick, D. (1992). Language and behavioral concerns for drug-exposed infants and toddlers. *Infant Toddler Intervention, 2*, 63.

Roberts, J. & Crais, E. (1989). Assessing communication skills. In D. Bailey & M. Wolery (Eds.), *Assessing infants and preschoolers with handicaps* (p. 98). Columbus, OH: Merrill.

Rossetti, L. (1990a). *Infant-toddler assessment: An interdisciplinary approach*. Boston: Little, Brown & Company.

Rossetti, L. (1990b). *The Rossetti infant-toddler language scale: A measure of communication and interaction*. East Moline, IL: LinguiSystems.

Rossetti, L. M. (2001). *Communication intervention: Birth to three*. Albany: Delmar Publishing.

Roth, F. & Spekman, N. (1984). Assessing the pragmatic abilities of children: Part 1. Organizational framework and assessment parameters. *Journal of Speech and Hearing Disorders, 49*, 2-11.

Sameroff, A. & Fiese, B. (1990). The social context of development. In N. Eisenburg (Ed.), *Contemporary topics in development*. New York: John Wiley & Sons.

Sander, E. (1972). When are speech sounds learned? *Journal of Speech & Hearing Disorders, 37*, 55-63.

Scherer, N. J., & D'Antonio, L. L. (1995). Parent questionnaire for screening early development in children with cleft palate. *Cleft Palate Craniofacial Journal, 32*, 1, 7-13.

Schlesinger, I. (1971). Production of utterances and language acquisition. In D. Slobin (Ed.), *The onogenesis of grammar*. New York: Academic Press.

Schultz, F. (1984). Fetal alcohol syndrome. In J. Blackman (Ed.), *Medical aspects of developmental disabilities in children birth to three*. Rockville, MD: Aspen Publishers.

Seligman, M. (1975). *Helplessness: On depression, development, and death*. San Francisco: W. H. Freeman.

Sevcik, R. A., Romski, M. A., & Wilkinson, K. M. (1991). Roles of graphic symbols in the language acquisition process for persons with severe cognitive disabilities. *Augmentative and Alternative Communication, 7*, 161-170.

Shonkoff, J. P., Hauser-Cram, P., Krauss, M. W., & Upshur, C. C. (1992). Development of infants with disabilities and their families. *Monographs of the Society for Research in Child Development, 57*, 6, (Serial No. 230).

Shprintzen, R. J. (1997). *Genetics, syndromes and communication disorders*. San Diego: Singular Publishing Group.

Siegel, L. (1983). Correction for prematurity and its consequences for the assessment of the very low birth weight infant. *Child Development, 54*, 1174.

Silberg, J. (2001). *Games to play with babies*. Beltsville, MD: Gryphon House, Inc.

Silberg, J. (2002). *Games to play with two-year-olds*. Beltsville, MD: Gryphon House, Inc.

Simeonsson, R. J. (1988). Evaluation of the effects of family-focused intervention. In D. Bailey and R. Simeonsson (Eds.), *Family assessment in early intervention* (p. 251-267). Columbus, OH: Charles E. Merrill.

Simon, B. M. & McGowan, J. S. (1989). Tracheostomy in young children: Implications for assessment and treatment of communication and feeding disorders. *Infants and Young Children, 1*, 1-9.

Sparks, S., Clark, M., Oas, D., & Erickson, R. (1988). *Clinical services to infants at risk for communication disorders*. Paper presented at the annual convention of the American Speech-Language-Hearing Association, Boston.

Spiker, D. & Hopmann, M. R. (1997). The effectiveness of early intervention for children with Down syndrome In M. J. Guralnick (Ed.), *The effectiveness of early intervention*. Baltimore: Paul H. Brookes Publishing Co.

Stark, R. E. (1995). Early language intervention: When, why, how? In J. A. Blackman (Ed.), *Treatment options in early intervention*. Gaithersburg, MD: Aspen Publishers.

Stark, R. E., Ansel, B. M., & Bond, J. (1988). Are pre-linguistic abilities predictive of learning disability? In M.A. Masland & R. L. Masland (Eds.), *Preschool prevention of reading failure*. Parkton, MD: York Press.

Stoel-Gammon, C. (1985). Phonetic inventories, 15-24 months: A longitudinal study. *Journal of Speech and Hearing Research, 28*, 506-512.

Stoel-Gammon, C. (1989). Prespeech and early speech development of two late talkers. *First Language, 9*, 207-224.

Stoel-Gammon, C. (1994). Normal and disordered phonology in two-year-olds. In K. G. Butler (Ed.), *Early intervention I: Working with infants and toddlers*. Gaithersburg, MD: Aspen Publishers.

Stoel-Gammon, C. & Dunn, C. (1985). *Normal and disordered phonology in children*. Baltimore: University Park Press.

Swigert, N. (1998). *The source for pediatric dysphagia*. East Moline, IL: LinguiSystems, Inc.

Theadore, G., Maher, S. R, & Prizant, B. M. (1994). Early assessment and intervention with emotional and behavioral disorders and communication disorders. In K. G. Butler (Ed.), *Early intervention I: Working with infants and toddlers*. Gaithersburg, MD: Aspen Publishers.

Trevarthen, C., Aitken, K., Papoudi, D., and Robarts, J. (1996). *Children with autism: Diagnosis and interventions to meet their needs*. London, England: Jessica Kingley Publishers.

Tyack, D. & Ingram, D. (1977). Children's production and comprehension of questions. *Journal of Child Language, 4*, 211-224.

Van Tatenhove, G. M. (1987). Teaching power through augmentative communication: Guidelines for early intervention. *Journal of Childhood Communication Disorders, 10*, 185-199.

Vygotsky, L. (1978). *Mind in society*. Cambridge, MA: Harvard University Press.

Ward, S. (1999). An investigation into the effectiveness of an early intervention method for the delayed language development in young children. *International Journal of Language and Communication Disorders, 34*, 243-264.

Warfield, M. E. (1995). The cost-effectiveness of home visiting versus group services in early intervention. *Journal of Early Intervention, 19*, 2, 130-148.

Warren, S. F., Yoder, P. J., Gazdag, G. E., Kim, K., & Jones, H. A. (1993). Facilitating pre-linguistic communication skills in young children with developmental delay. *Journal of Speech and Hearing Research, 36*, 83-97.

Warren, S. & Kaiser, A. (1986). Incidental language teaching: A critical review. *Journal of Speech and Hearing Disorders, 51*, 291-299.

Westby, C. (1980). Assessment of language and cognitive abilities through play. *Language, Speech, and Hearing Services in Schools, 3*, 154.

Wetherby, A., Cain, D., Yonclas, D., & Walker, V. (1988). Analysis of intentional communication of normal children from the pre-linguistic to the multi-word stage. *Journal of Speech and Hearing Research, 31*, 240.

Wetherby, A. & Prizant, B. (1992). Profiling young children's communicative competence. In S. Warren & J. Reichle (Eds.), *Causes and effects in communication and language intervention* (pp. 217-253). Baltimore: Paul H. Brookes Publishing Co.

Wetherby, A. M. & Prizant, B. M. (2003). *Communication and symbolic behavior scales-CSBS manual*. Baltimore, MD: Paul H. Brookes Publishing Co.

Whitehurst, G. J., Fisher, J. E., Lonigan, C. J., Valdez-Menchaca, M. C., Arnold, D. S., & Smith, M. (1991). Treatment of early expressive language delay: If, when, and how. *Topics in Language Disorders, 11*, 4, 55-68.

Wilcox, M. J., Kouri, T. A., & Caswell, S. B. (1991). Early intervention: A comparison of classroom and individual treatment. *American Journal of Speech-Language Pathology, 1*, 1, 49-62.

Yoder, P. (1999). Letter to the editor. *International Journal of Language and Communication Disorders. 34*, 4, 441-444.

Yoder, P., Kaiser, A., & Alpert, C. (1991). An exploratory study of the interaction between language teaching methods and child characteristics. *Journal of Speech and Hearing Research, 34*, 155-167.

Yoder, P. & Warren, S. (1993). Can developmentally delayed children's language development be enhanced through pre-linguistic intervention? In A. Kaiser & D. Gray (Eds.), *Enhancing children's communication: Research foundations for intervention* (p.120). Baltimore: Paul H. Brookes Publishing Co.

Yoder, P. J., Warren, S. F., Kim, K., & Gazdag, G. E. (1994). Facilitating pre-linguistic communication skills in young children with developmental delay II: Systematic replication and extension. *Journal of Speech and Hearing Research, 37*, 841-851.

Yoshinaga-Itano, C. (2000). The Colorado newborn hearing screening project: Effects on speech and language development for children with hearing loss. *Journal of Perinatology, 20,* 8, 132.

Yoshinaga-Itano, C. & Apuzzo, M. (1998a). Identification of hearing loss after age 18 months is not early enough. *American Annals of the Deaf, 143,* 380-387.

Yoshinaga-Itano, C. & Apuzzo, M. (1998b). The development of deaf and hard-of-hearing children identified early through the high-risk registry. *American Annals of the Deaf, 143,* 416-424.

Yoshinaga-Itano, C., Sedey, A. L., Coulter, D. K., & Mehl, A. L. (1998). The language of early- and later-identified children with hearing loss. *Pediatrics, 100,* 1161-1171.

Yovetich, W. S. & Young, T. A. (1988). The effects of representativeness and concreteness on the "guessability" of Blissymbols. *Augmentative and Alternative Communication, 4,* 35-39.

Zambone, A. (1995). Serving the young child with visual impairments: An overview of disability impact and intervention needs. In Blackman J. (Ed.), *Treatment options in early intervention.* Gaithersburg, MD: Aspen Publishers.

Ziev, M. S. (1999). Earliest intervention: Speech-language pathology services in the neonatal intensive care unit. *Asha, 41,* 3, 32-6.

Zimmerman, I. L., Steiner, V. G., & Pond, R. E. (2002). *Preschool language scale–Fourth edition.* San Antonio, TX: The Psychological Corporation.